For those fighting the good fight, running the race, and those who stand courageously beside them. Uplifting quotes, Bible verses, and photography by Emily J Stauring to inspire the soul to never give up. All images by Emily J Stauring.

Kiss It Cancer
ISBN: 978-0-578-14927-1

First Edition
Publisher: Emily J Photo Decor
Printed in the United States Of America

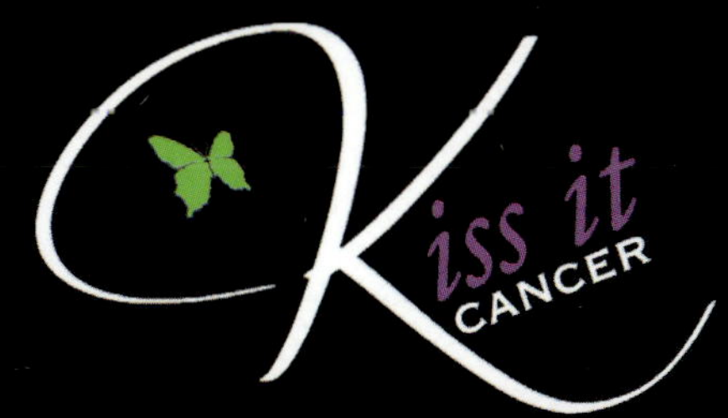

WWW.KISSITCANCER.COM

A portion of the proceeds from sales of this book will help us to provide further inspirational donations to hospitals and patients in need across the country. *(Inspirational pictures, free books, etc)*

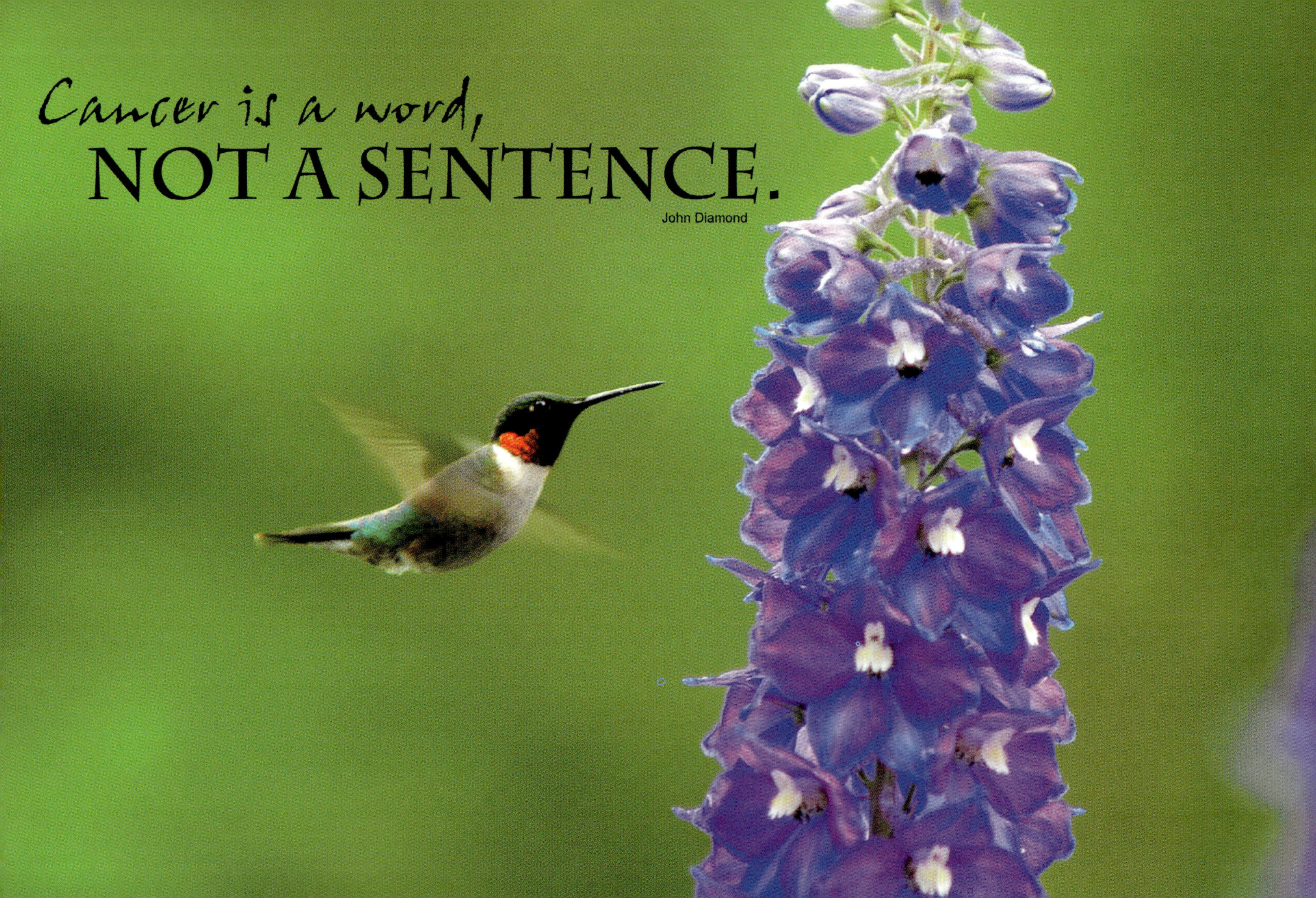
Cancer is a word,
NOT A SENTENCE.
John Diamond

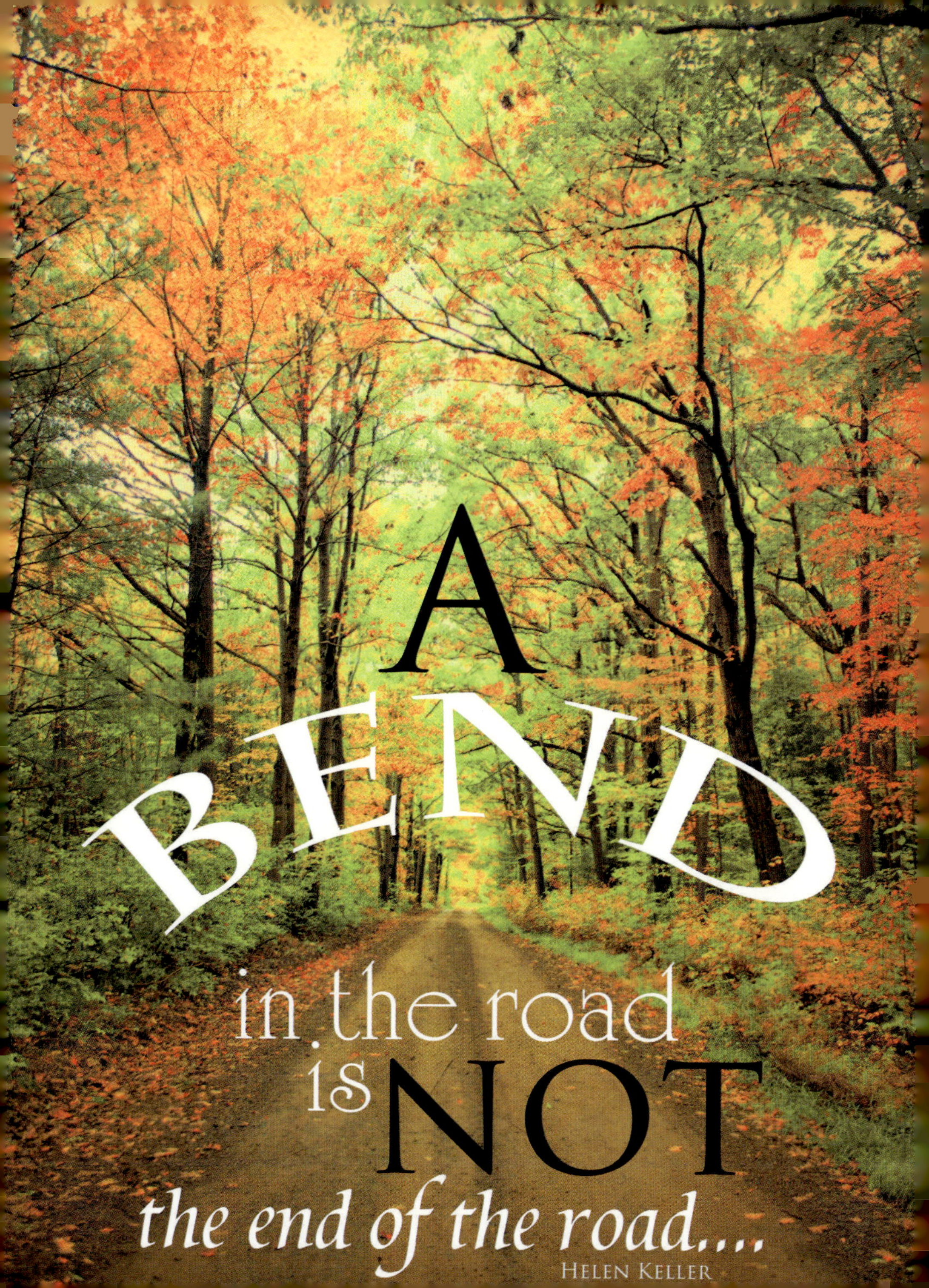
A
BEND
in the road
is NOT
the end of the road....
HELEN KELLER

Feed your FAITH
and your FEARS
will disappear.

AUTHOR UNKNOWN

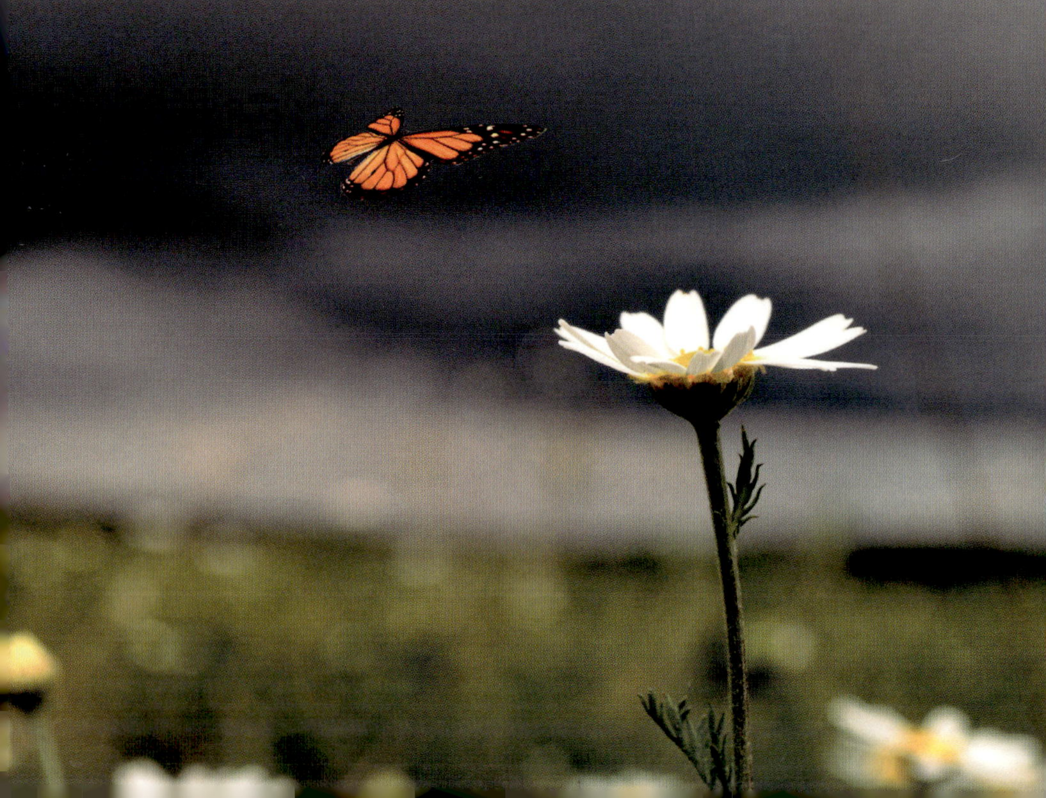

Your present circumstances don't determine
where
you can go;

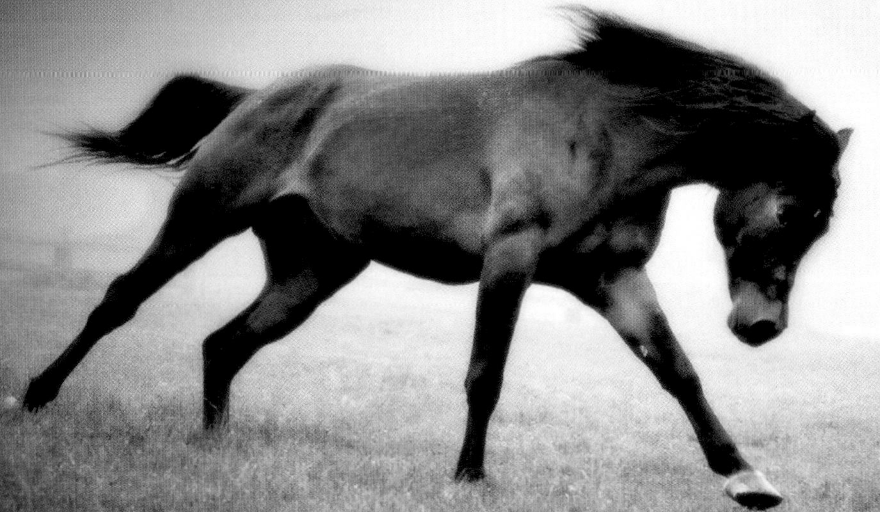

they merely determine where you
start.

Nido Qubein

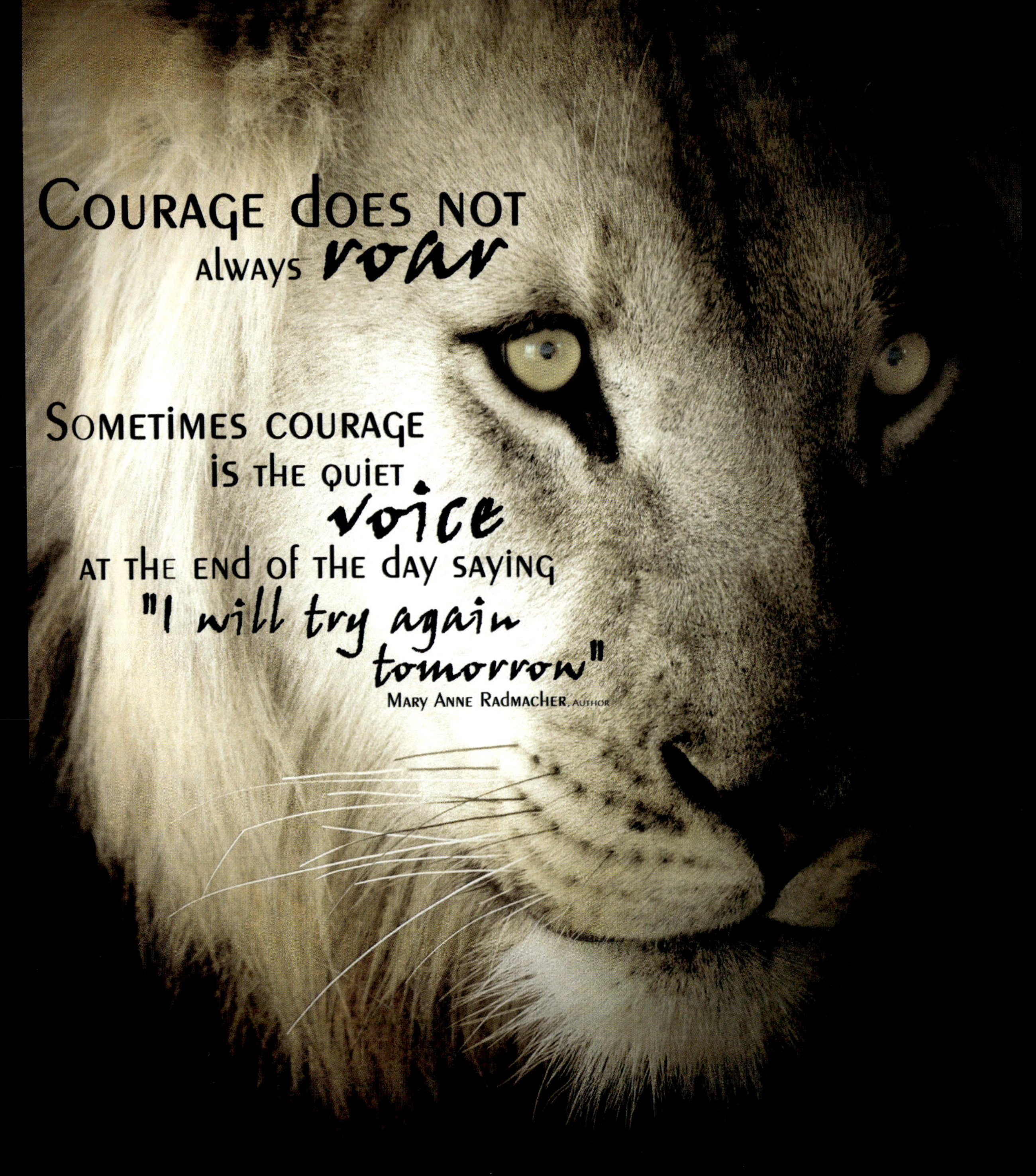
Courage does not
always roar
Sometimes courage
is the quiet
voice
at the end of the day saying
"I will try again
tomorrow"
Mary Anne Radmacher, author

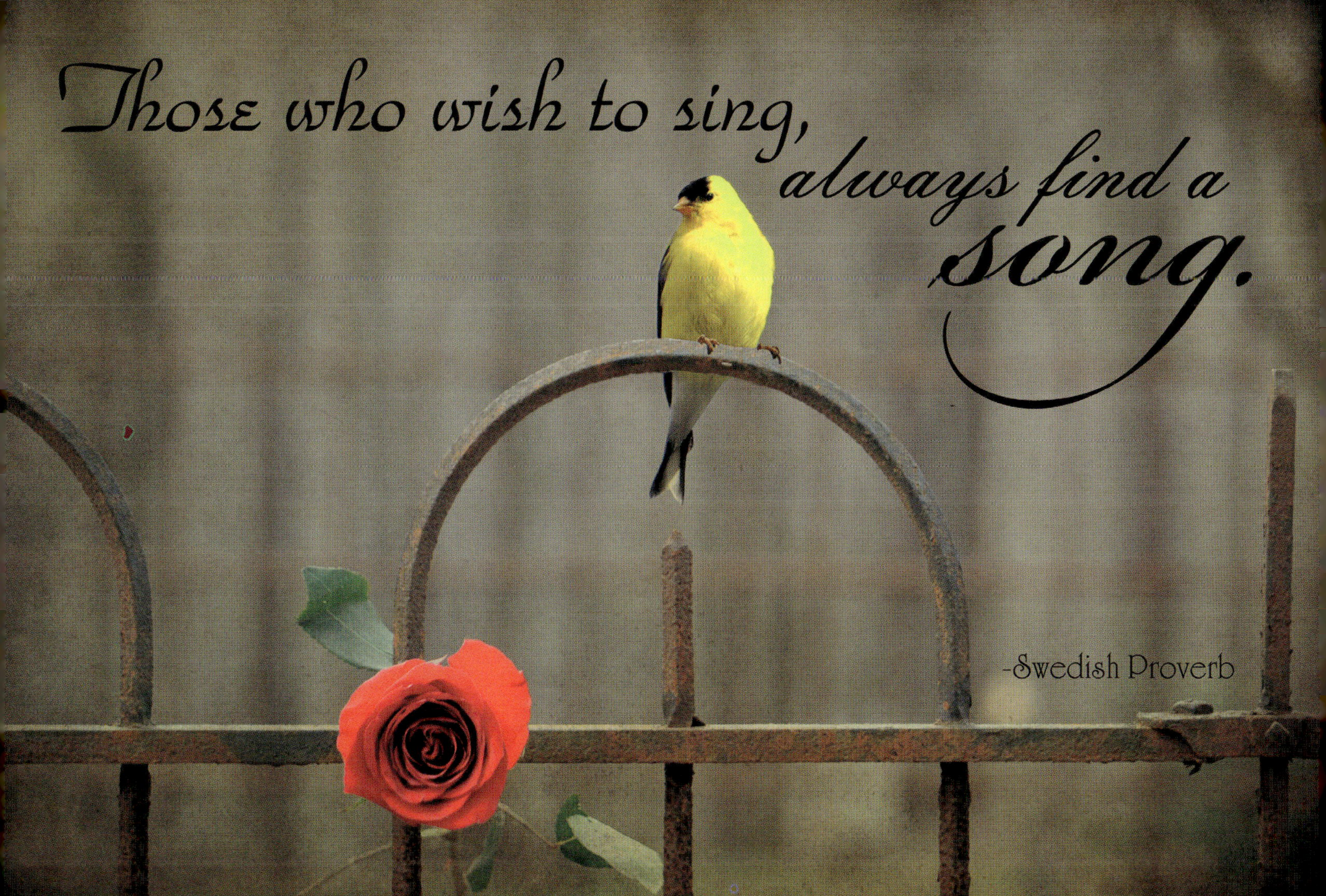
Those who wish to sing,
always find a
song.
-Swedish Proverb

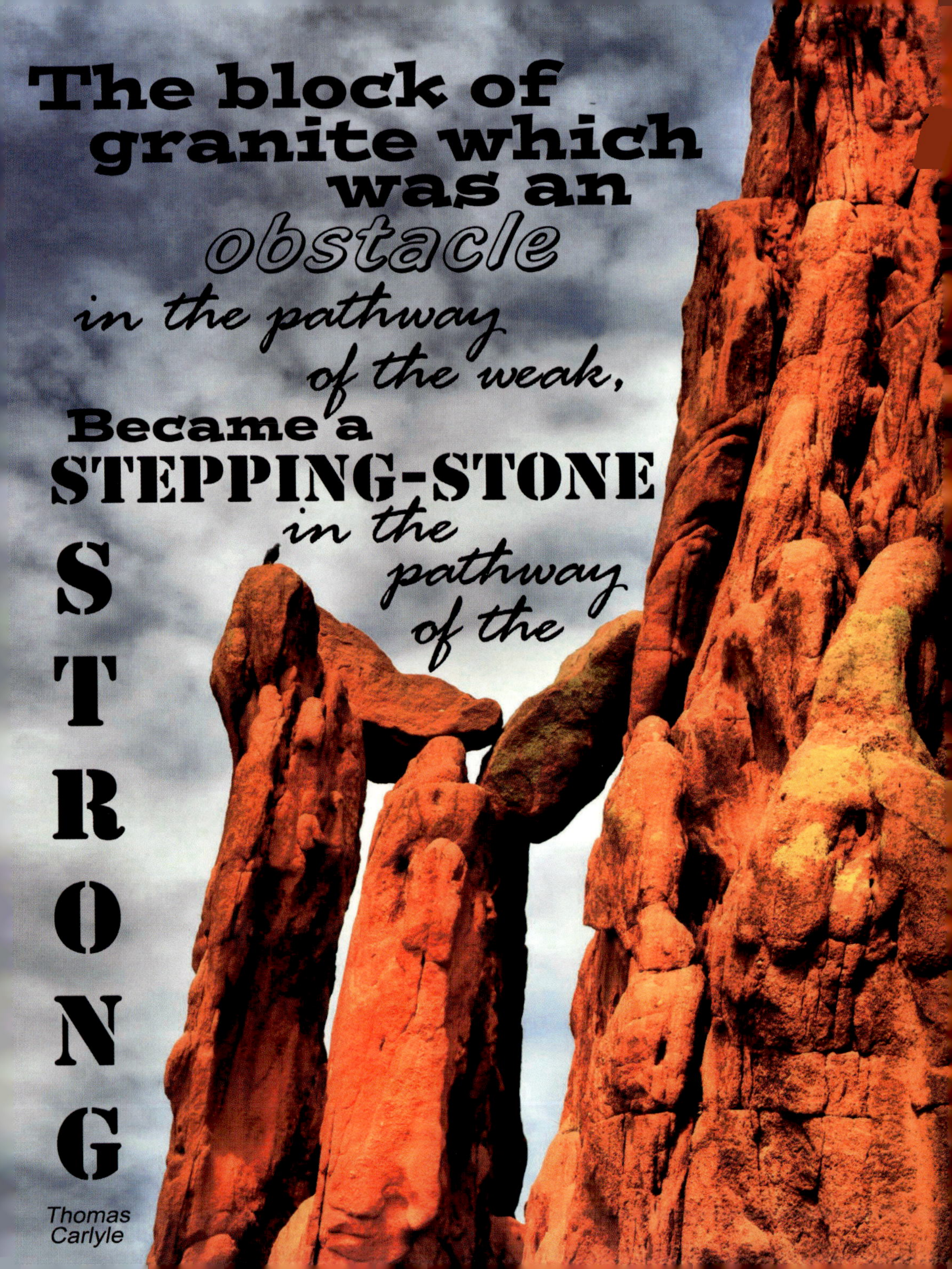
The block of
granite which
was an
obstacle
in the pathway
of the weak,
Became a
STEPPING-STONE
in the
pathway
of the
STRONG
Thomas
Carlyle

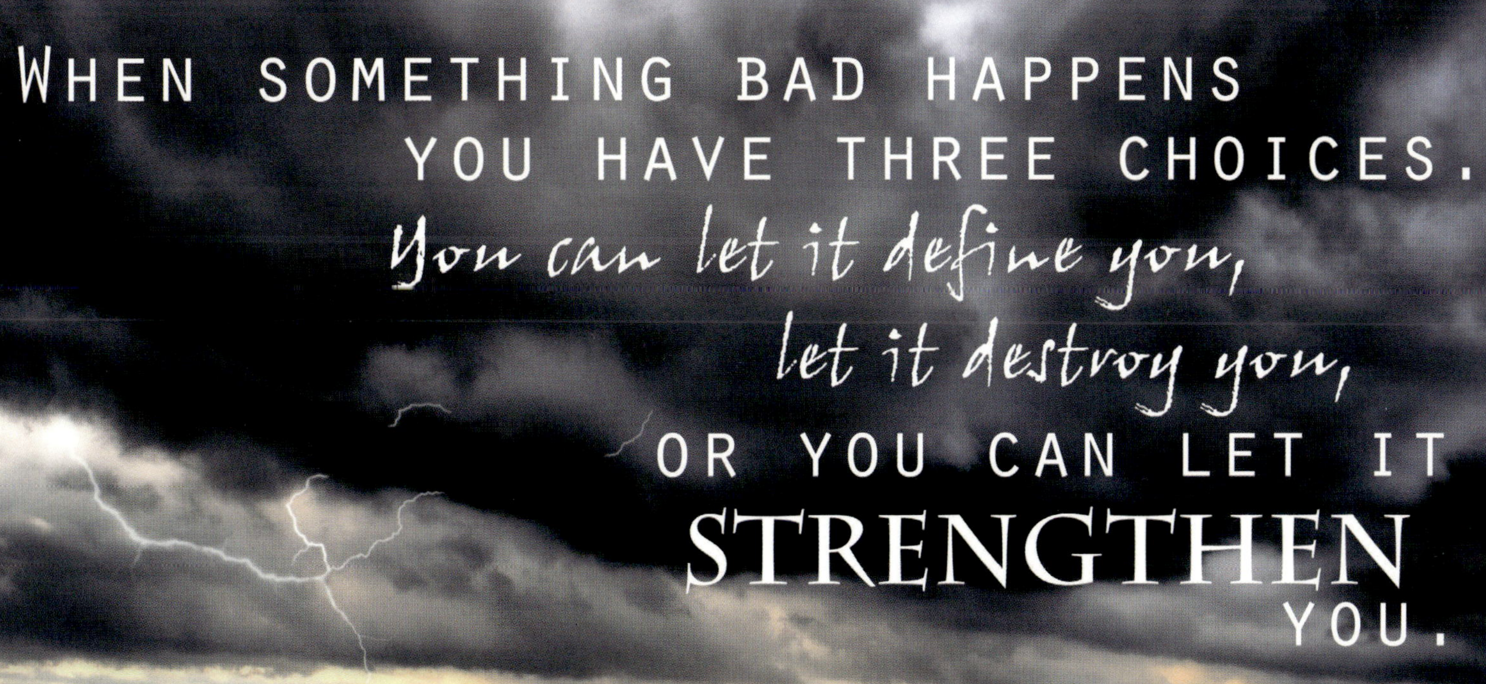
WHEN SOMETHING BAD HAPPENS
YOU HAVE THREE CHOICES.
You can let it define you,
let it destroy you,
OR YOU CAN LET IT
STRENGTHEN
YOU.
AUTHOR UNKNOWN

BLESSED

is the one who

PERSEVERES

UNDER TRIAL BECAUSE,
AFTER HAVING STOOD THE TEST,
THAT PERSON WILL RECEIVE THE
CROWN OF

LIFE

THAT THE LORD HAS PROMISED
TO THOSE WHO LOVE HIM.

JAMES 1:12

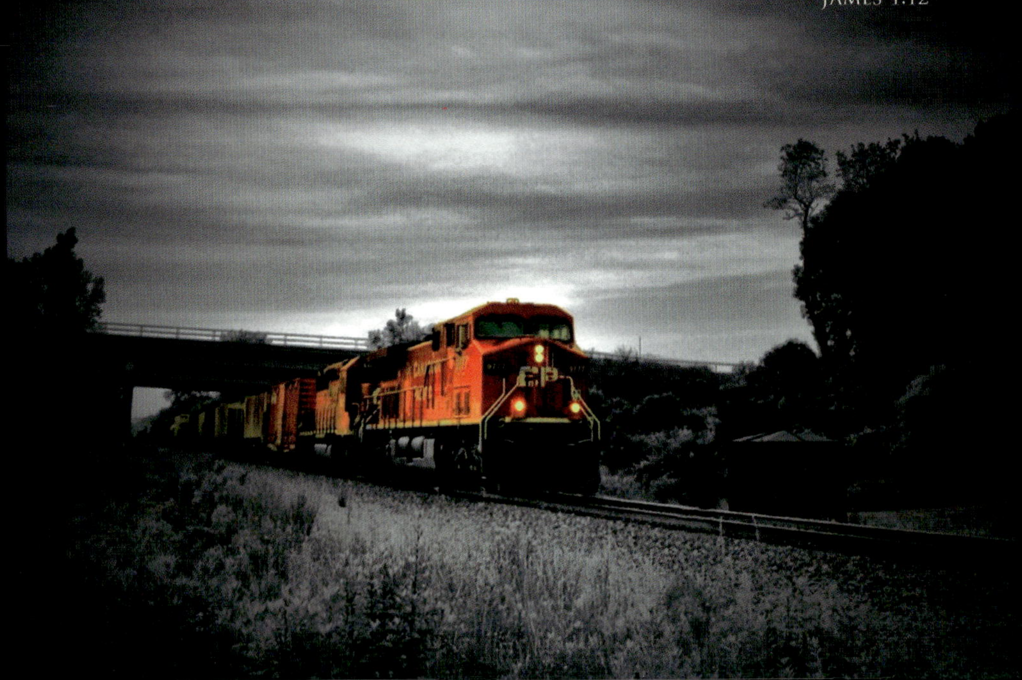

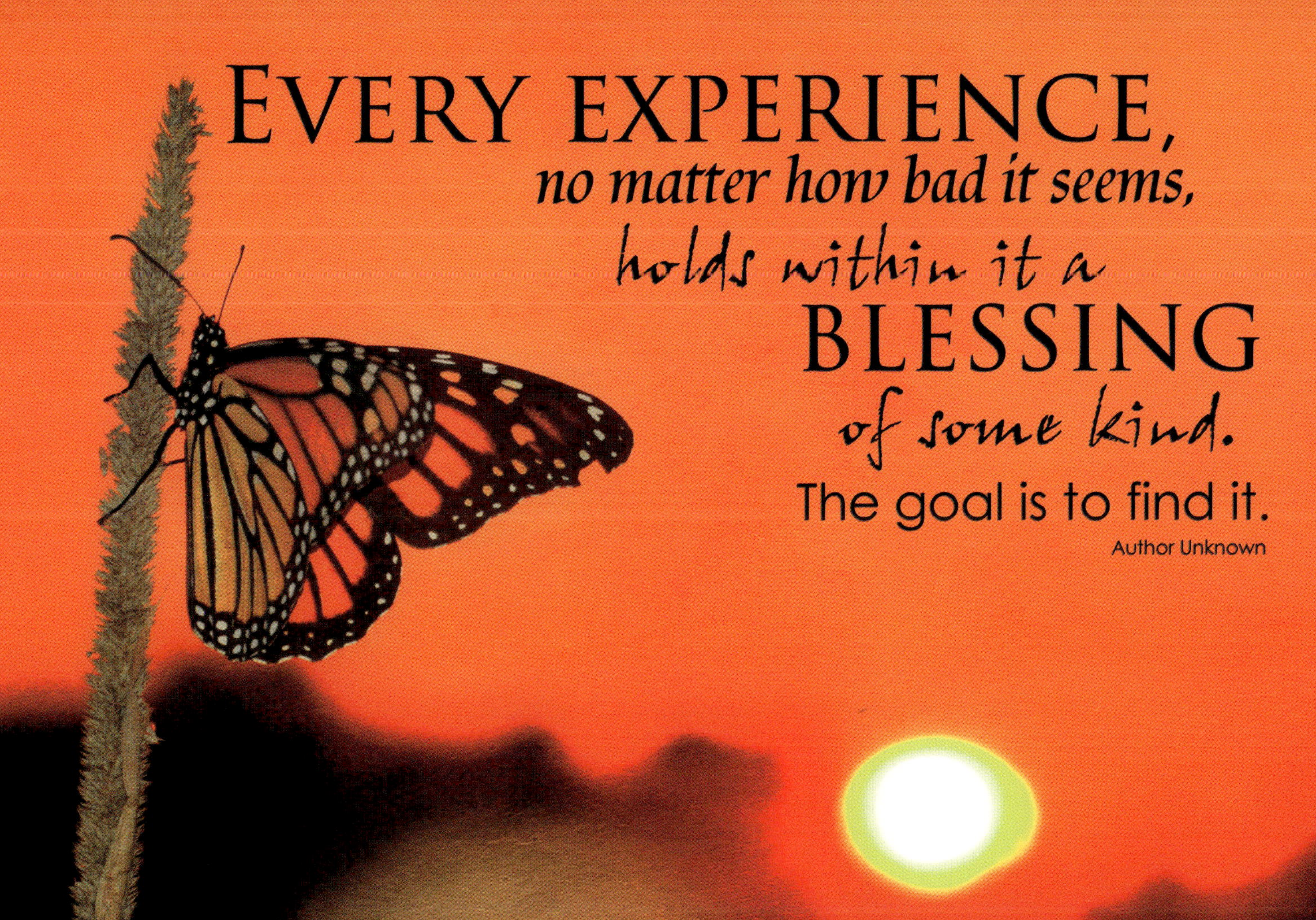
EVERY EXPERIENCE,
no matter how bad it seems,
holds within it a
BLESSING
of some kind.
The goal is to find it.
Author Unknown

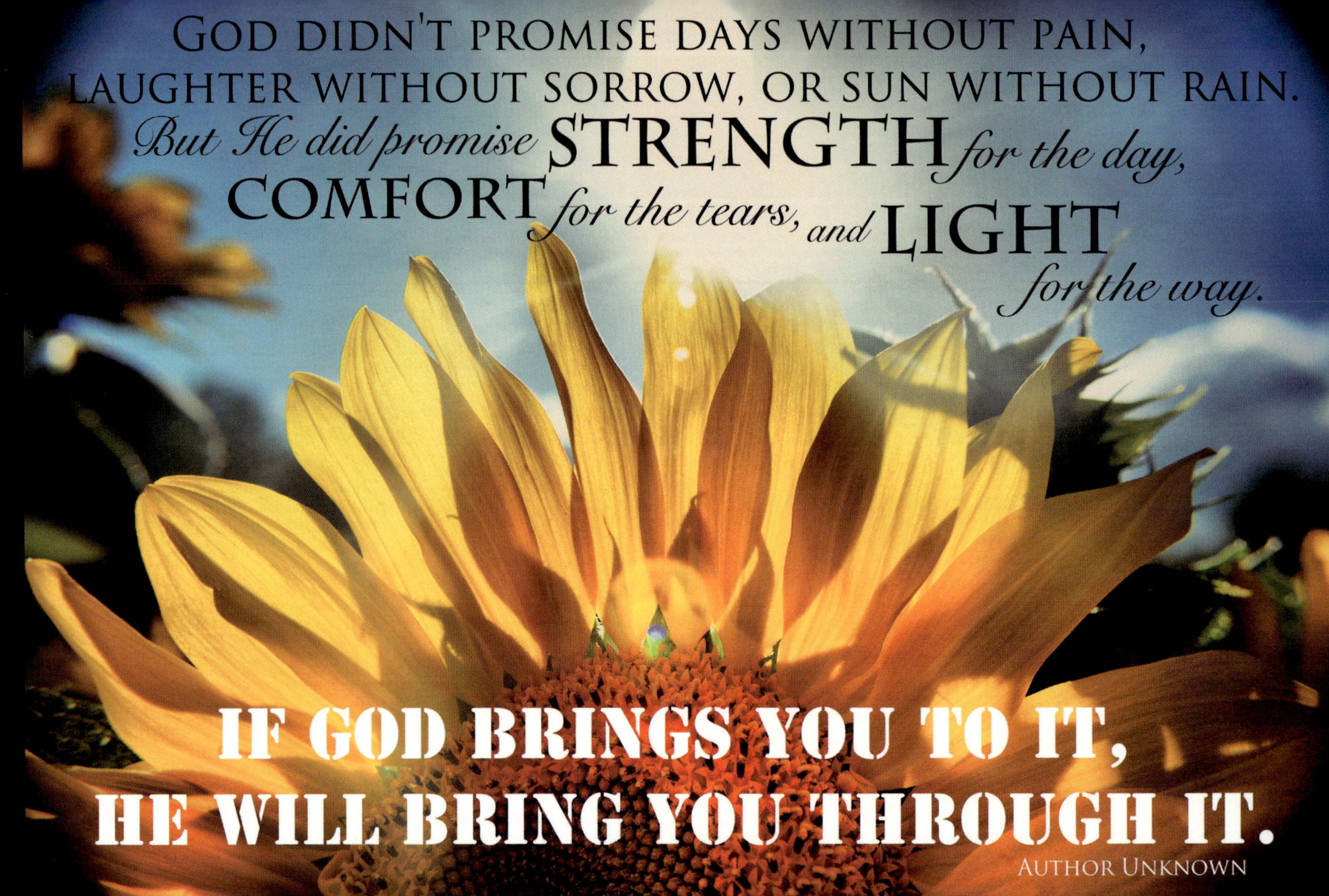
GOD DIDN'T PROMISE DAYS WITHOUT PAIN,
LAUGHTER WITHOUT SORROW, OR SUN WITHOUT RAIN.
But He did promise STRENGTH for the day,
COMFORT for the tears, and LIGHT
for the way.
IF GOD BRINGS YOU TO IT,
HE WILL BRING YOU THROUGH IT.
AUTHOR UNKNOWN

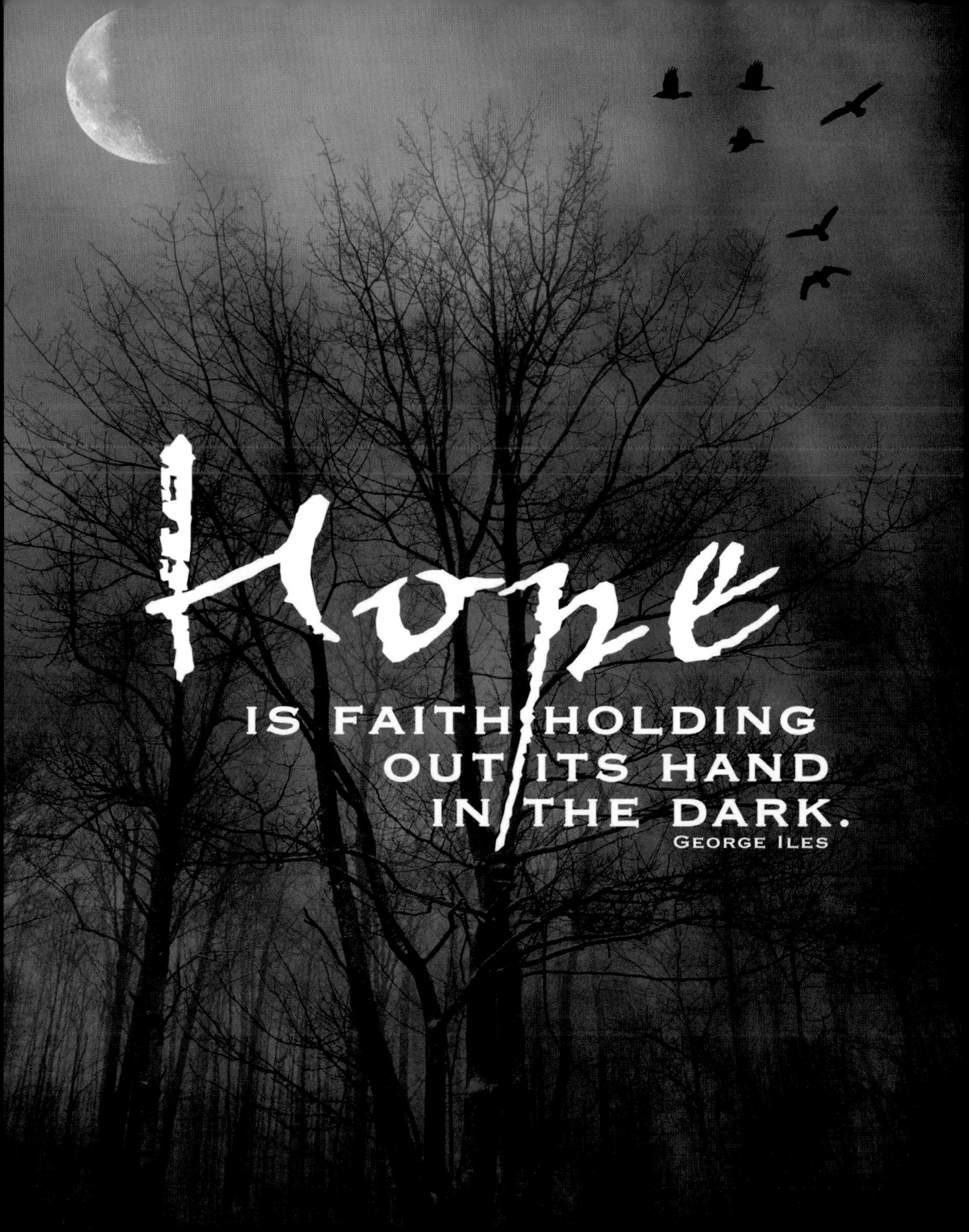

Hope

IS FAITH HOLDING
OUT ITS HAND
IN THE DARK.

George Iles

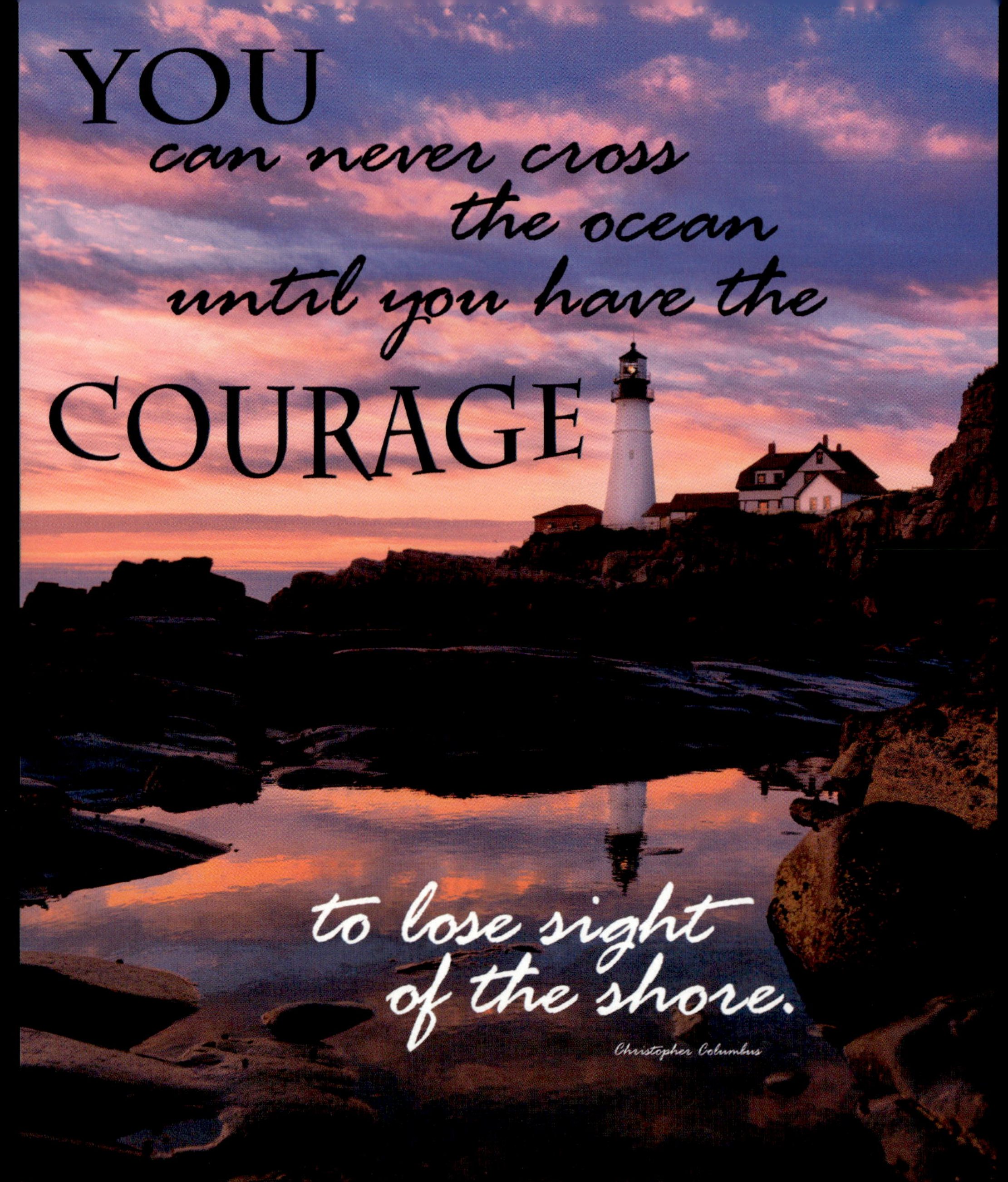
YOU
can never cross
the ocean
until you have the
COURAGE
to lose sight
of the shore.
Christopher Columbus

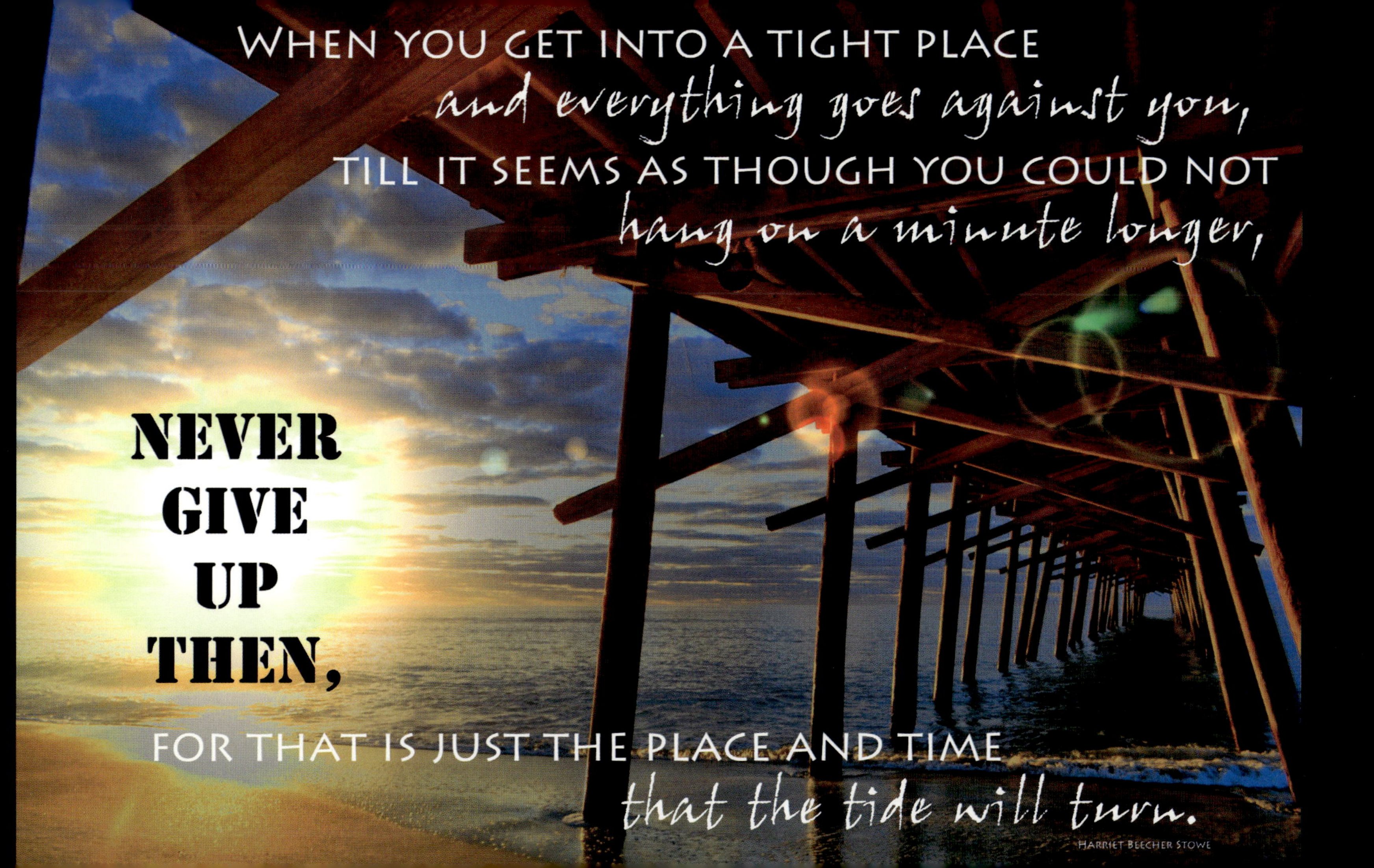

WHEN YOU GET INTO A TIGHT PLACE
and everything goes against you,
TILL IT SEEMS AS THOUGH YOU COULD NOT
hang on a minute longer,

NEVER GIVE UP THEN,

FOR THAT IS JUST THE PLACE AND TIME
that the tide will turn.

HARRIET BEECHER STOWE

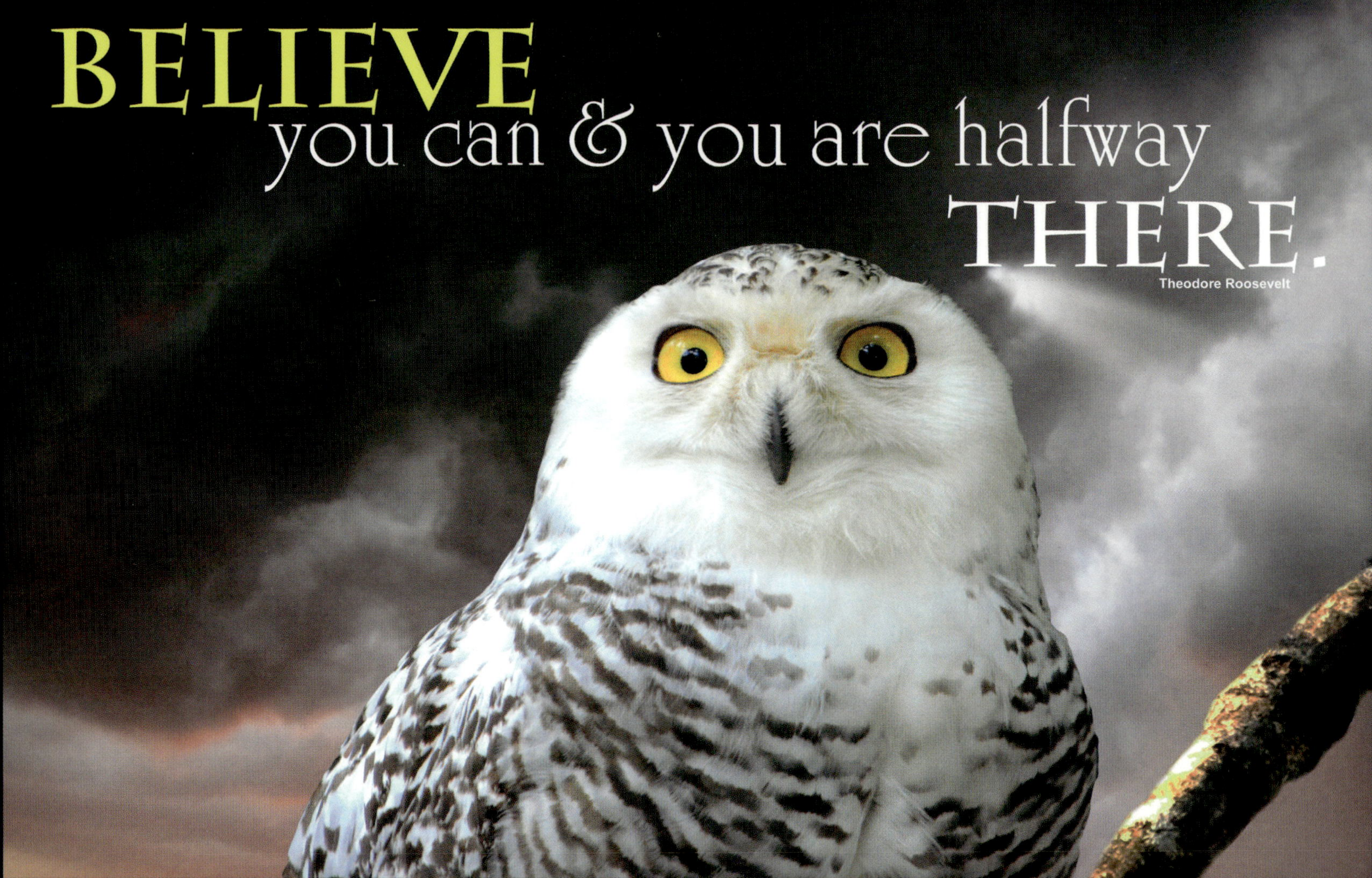
BELIEVE
you can & you are halfway
THERE.
Theodore Roosevelt

Strength does not come from physical capacity. It comes from an INDOMITABLE WILL.

Mahatma Gandhi

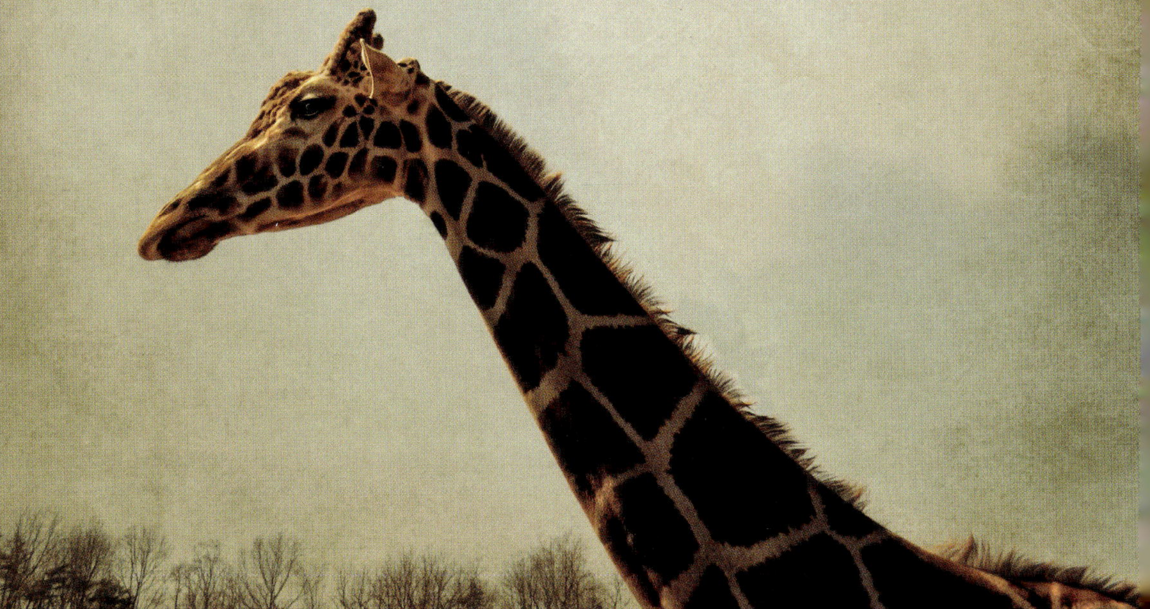

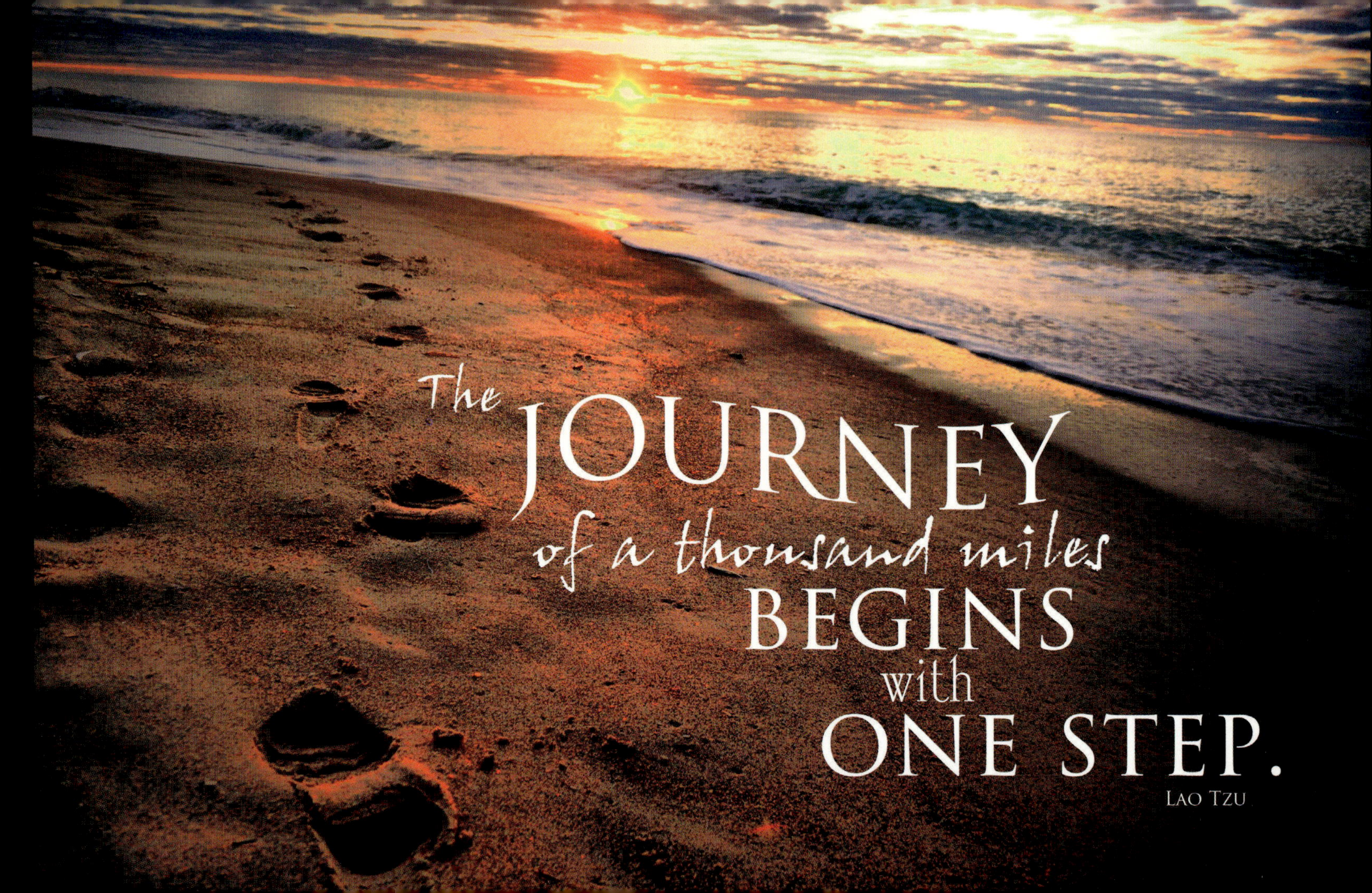
The
JOURNEY
of a thousand miles
BEGINS
with
ONE STEP.
LAO TZU

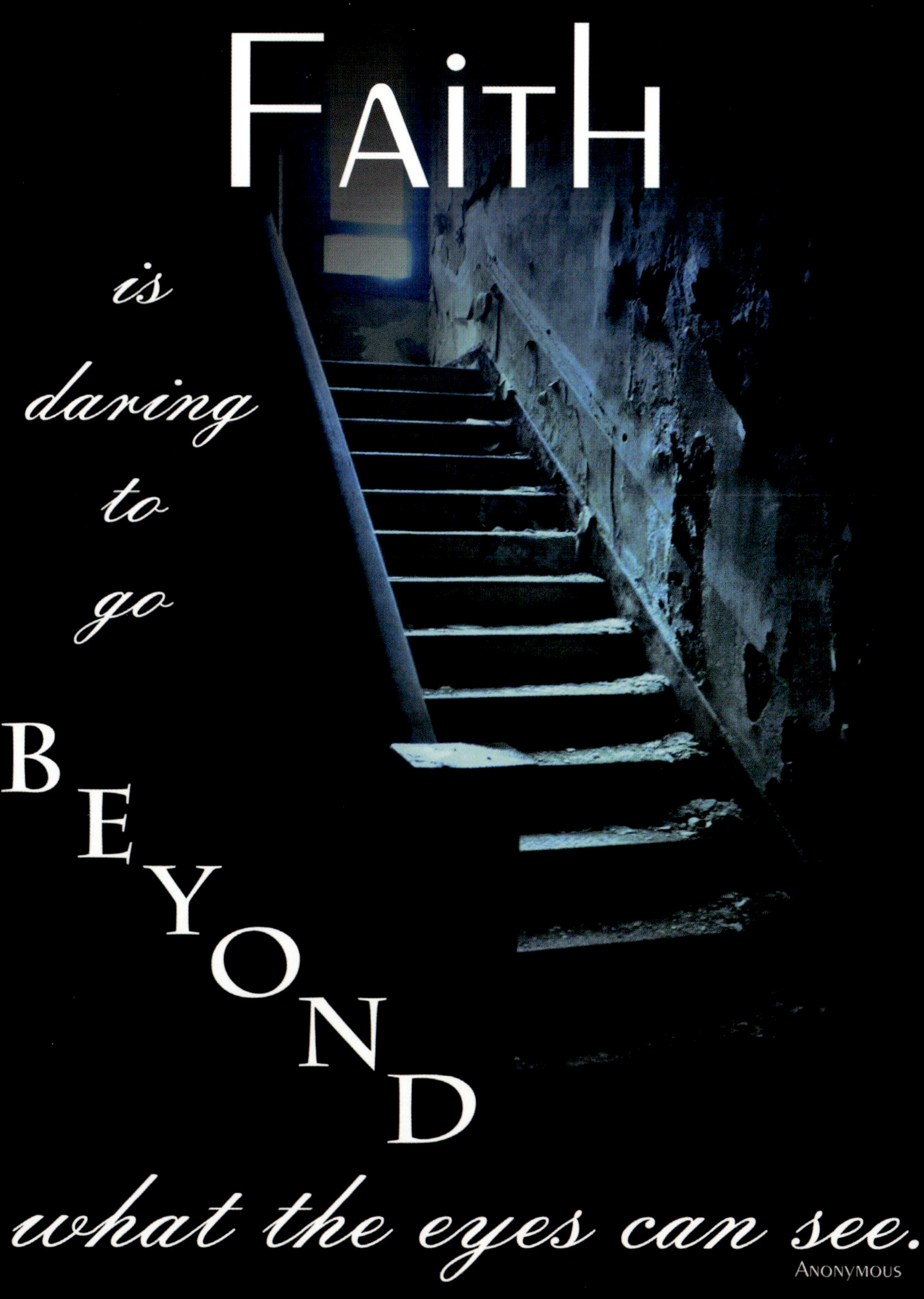
FAITH
is
daring
to
go
BEYOND
what the eyes can see.
ANONYMOUS

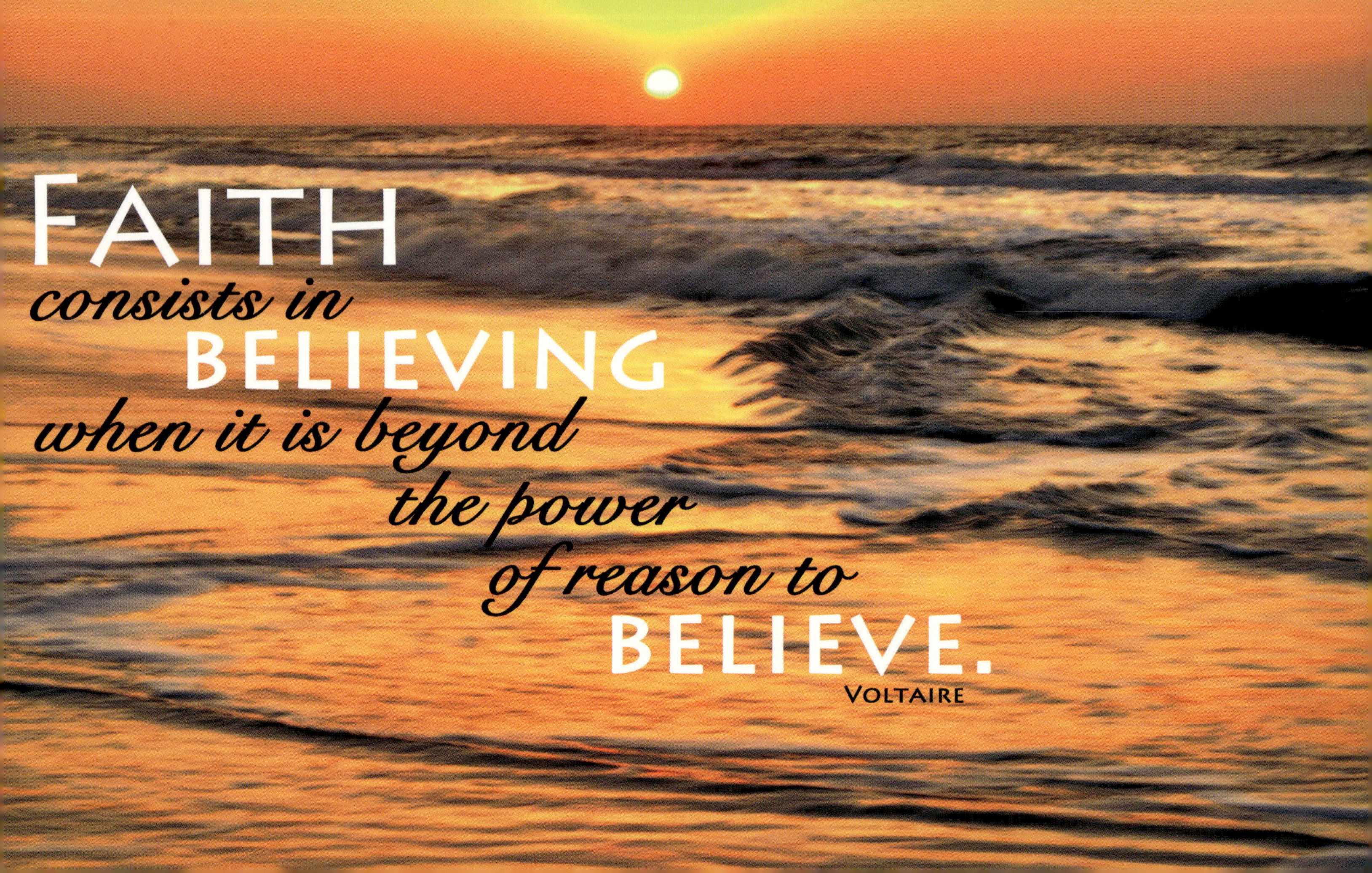
FAITH
consists in
BELIEVING
when it is beyond
the power
of reason to
BELIEVE.
VOLTAIRE

When you think about it, what other choice is there but

TO HOPE?

We have two options, medically & emotionally:

GIVE UP OR

fight like hell.

LANCE ARMSTRONG

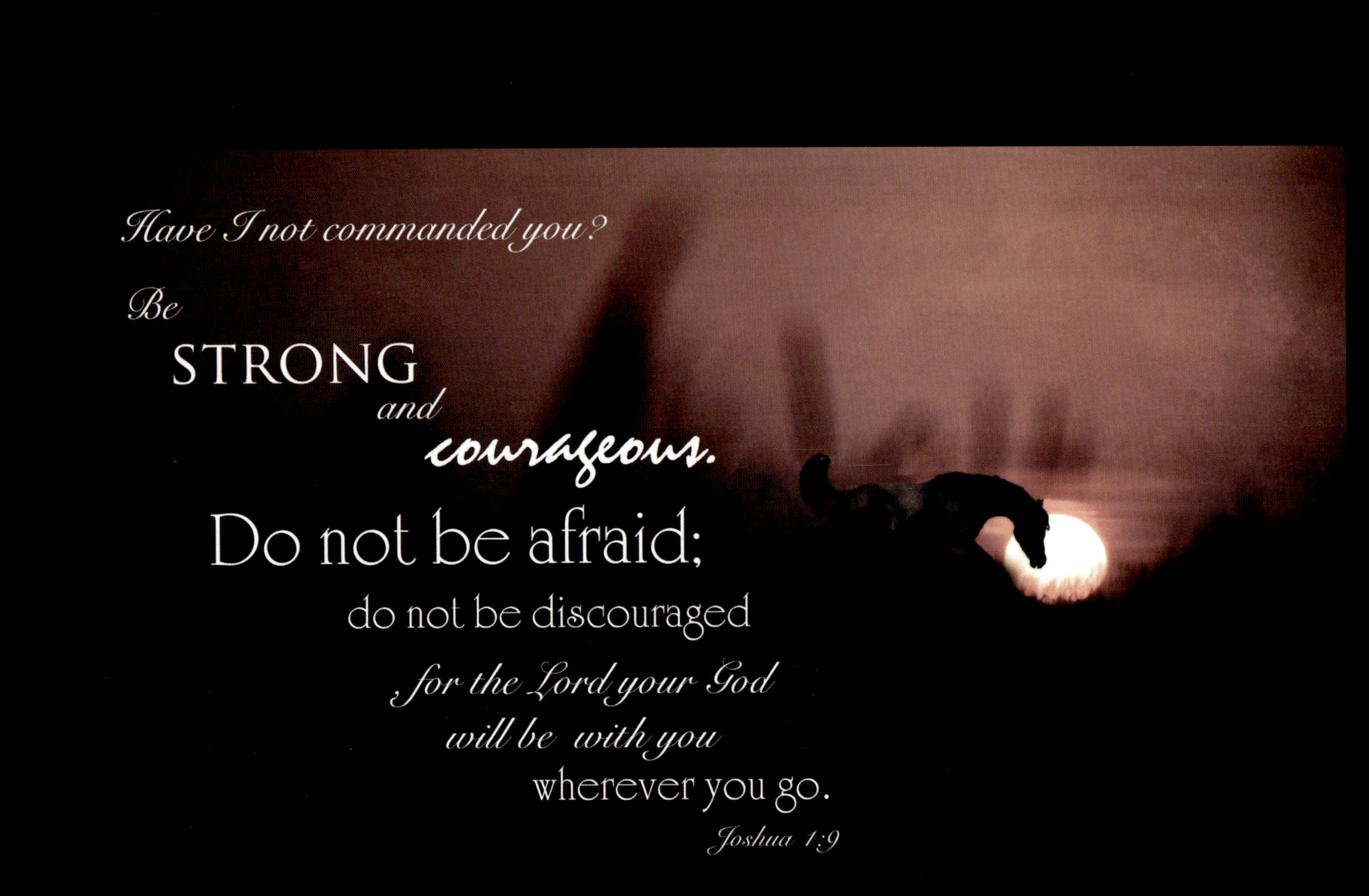

Have I not commanded you?

Be

STRONG

and

courageous.

Do not be afraid;

do not be discouraged

, for the Lord your God

will be with you

wherever you go.

Joshua 1:9

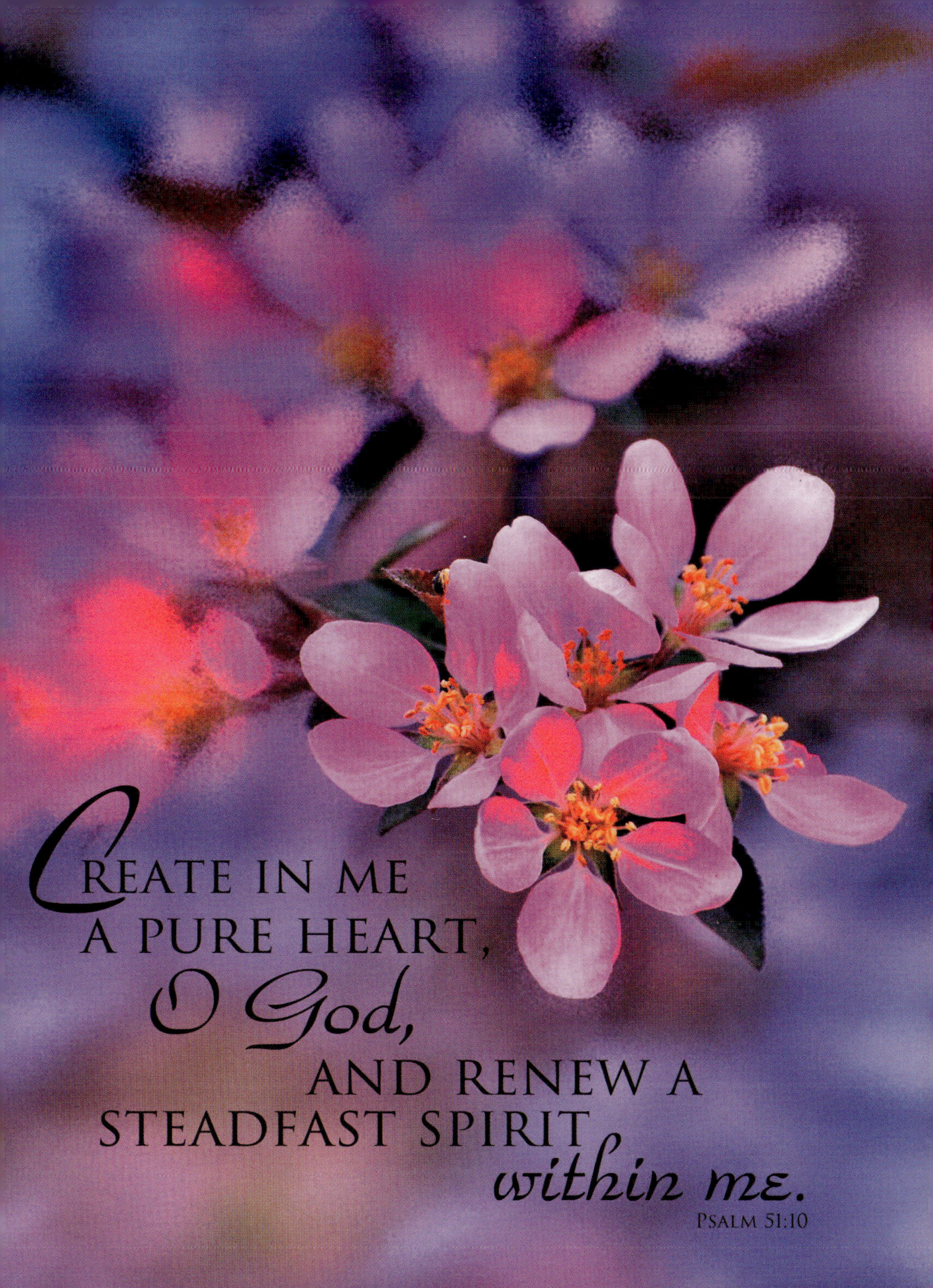
CREATE IN ME
A PURE HEART,
O God,
AND RENEW A
STEADFAST SPIRIT
within me.
PSALM 51:10

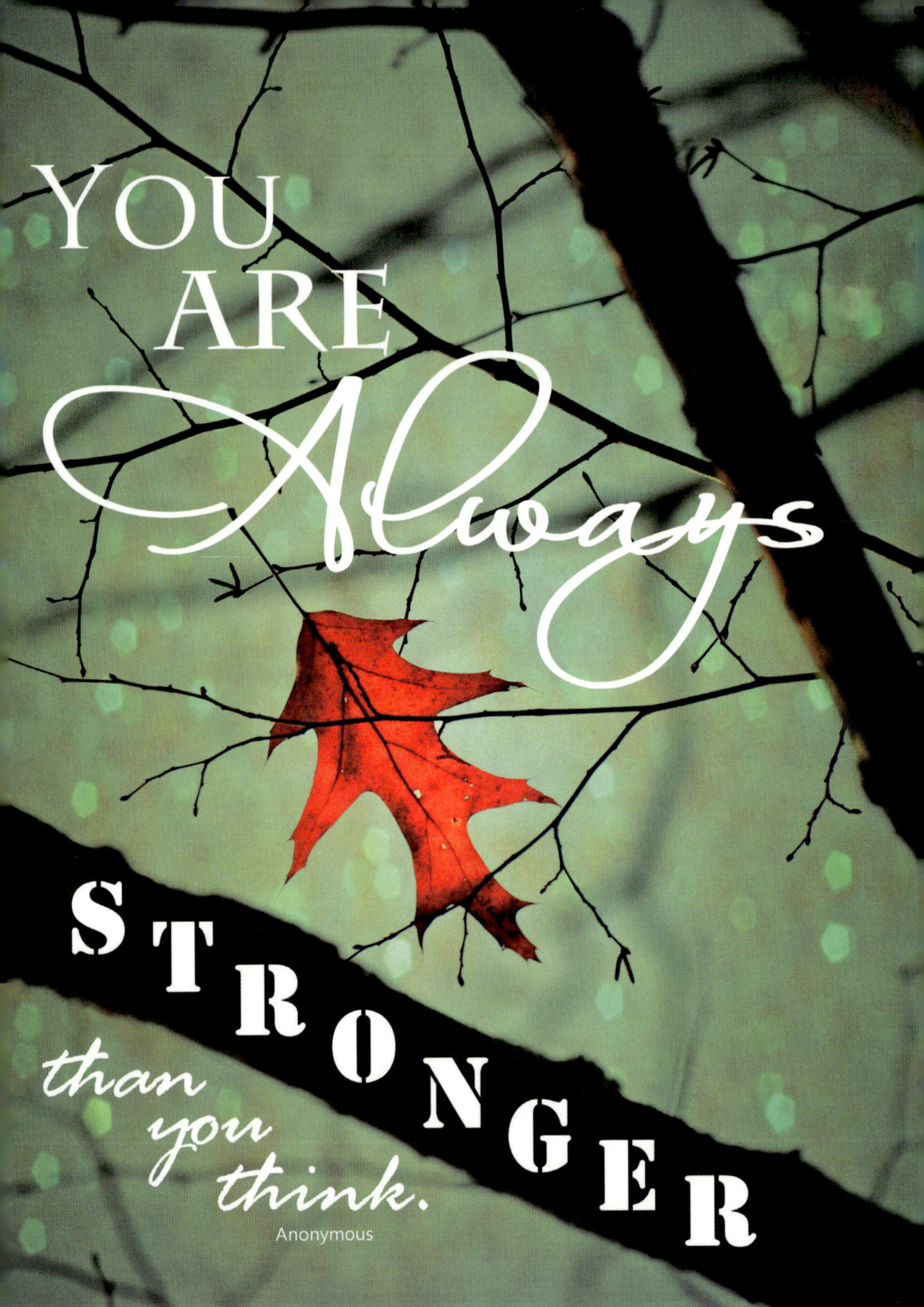
YOU
ARE
Always
STRONGER
than
you
think.
Anonymous

FAITH

is the substance of things

HOPED

for;

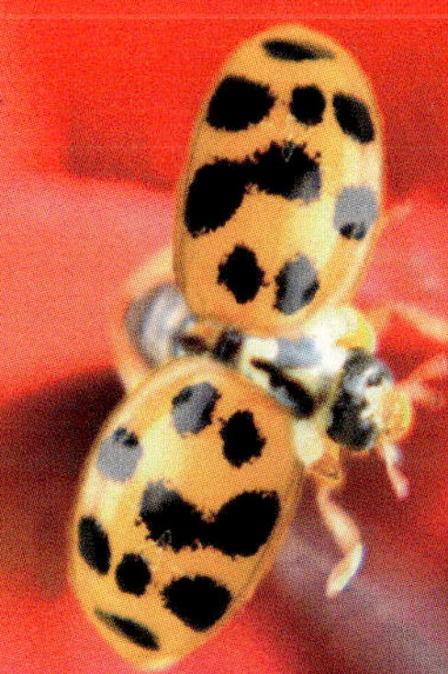

the

EVIDENCE

of things not seen.

Hebrews 11:1

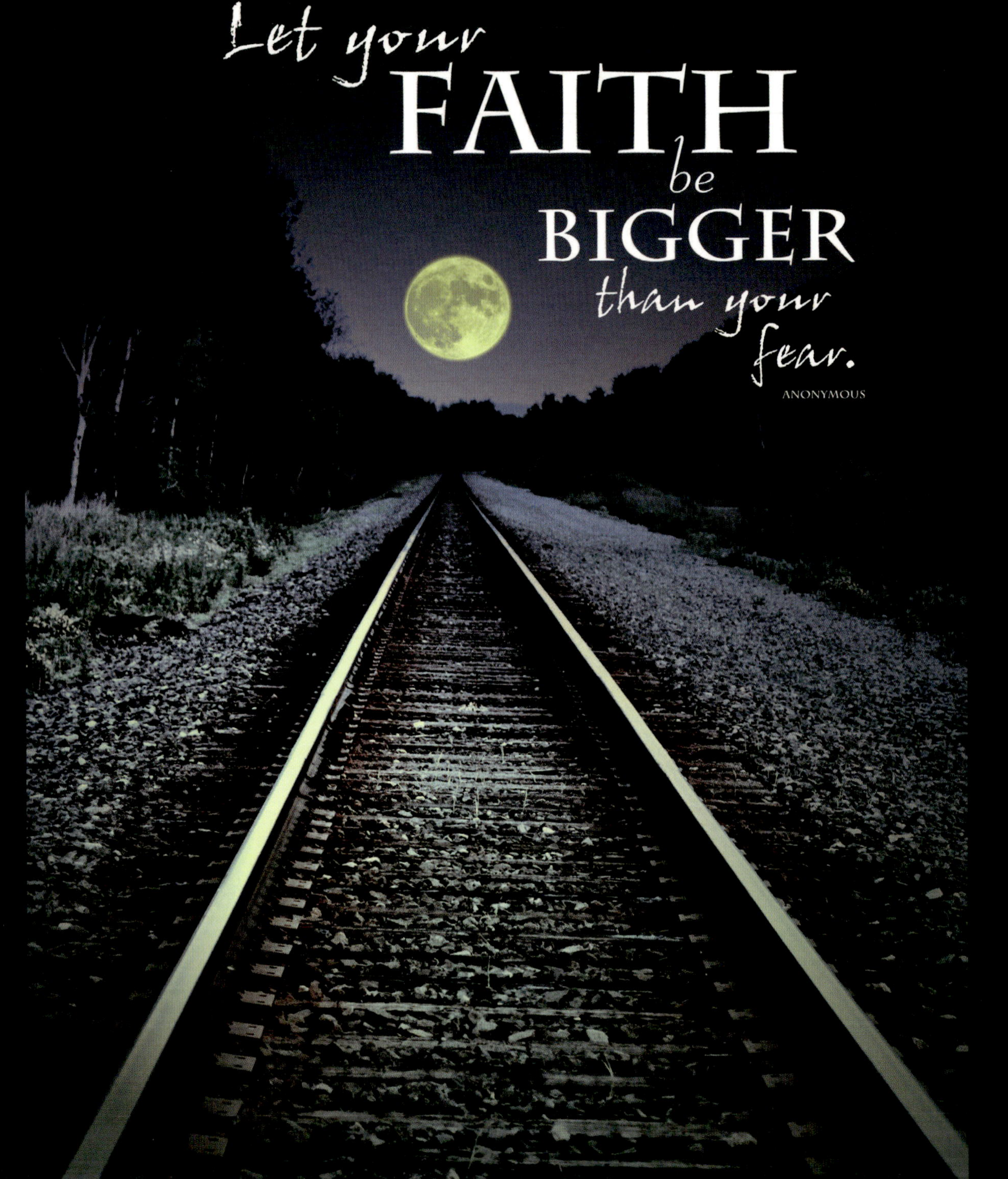
Let your
FAITH
be
BIGGER
than your
fear.
ANONYMOUS

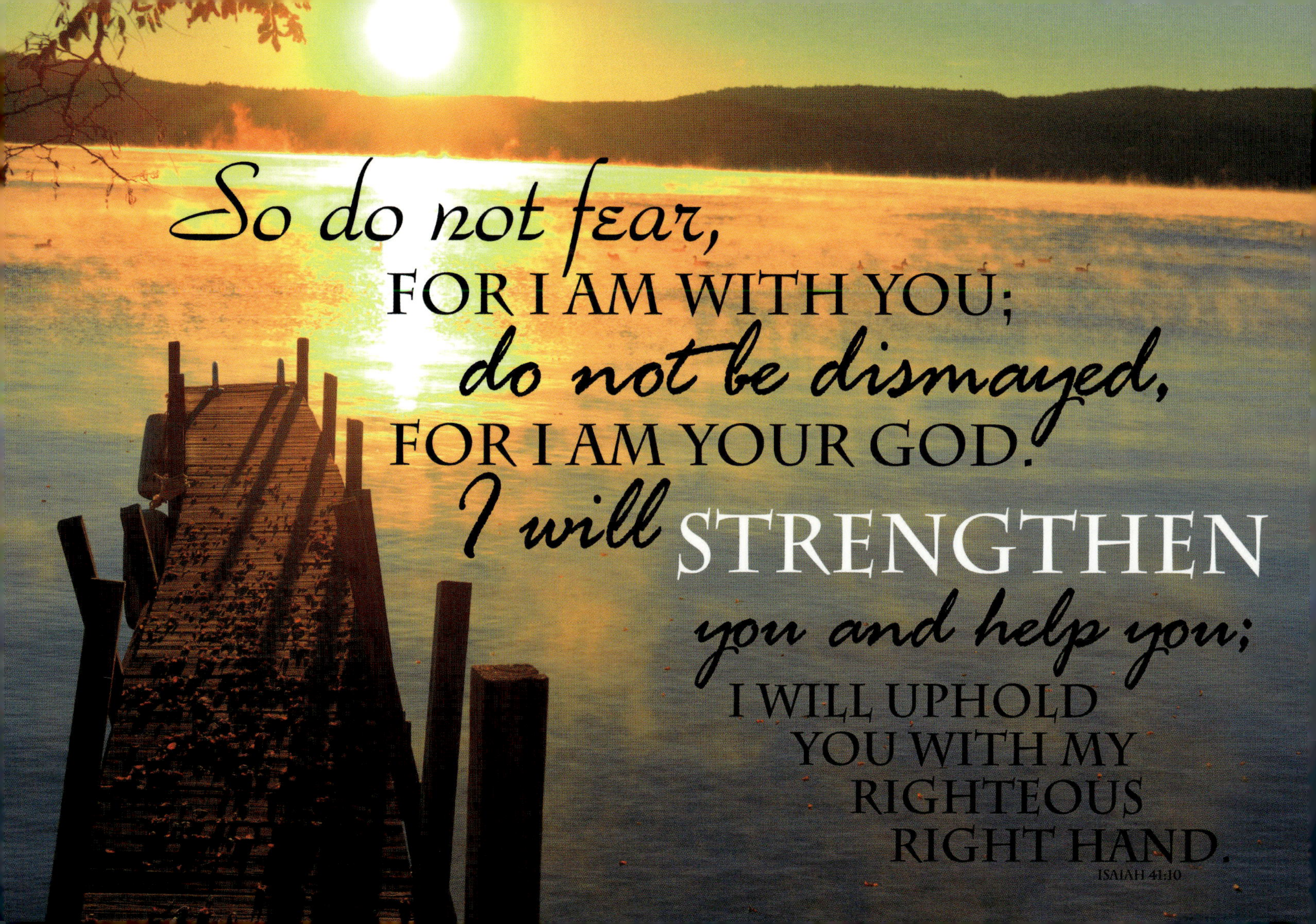
So do not fear,
FOR I AM WITH YOU;
do not be dismayed,
FOR I AM YOUR GOD.
I will STRENGTHEN
you and help you;
I WILL UPHOLD
YOU WITH MY
RIGHTEOUS
RIGHT HAND.
ISAIAH 41:10

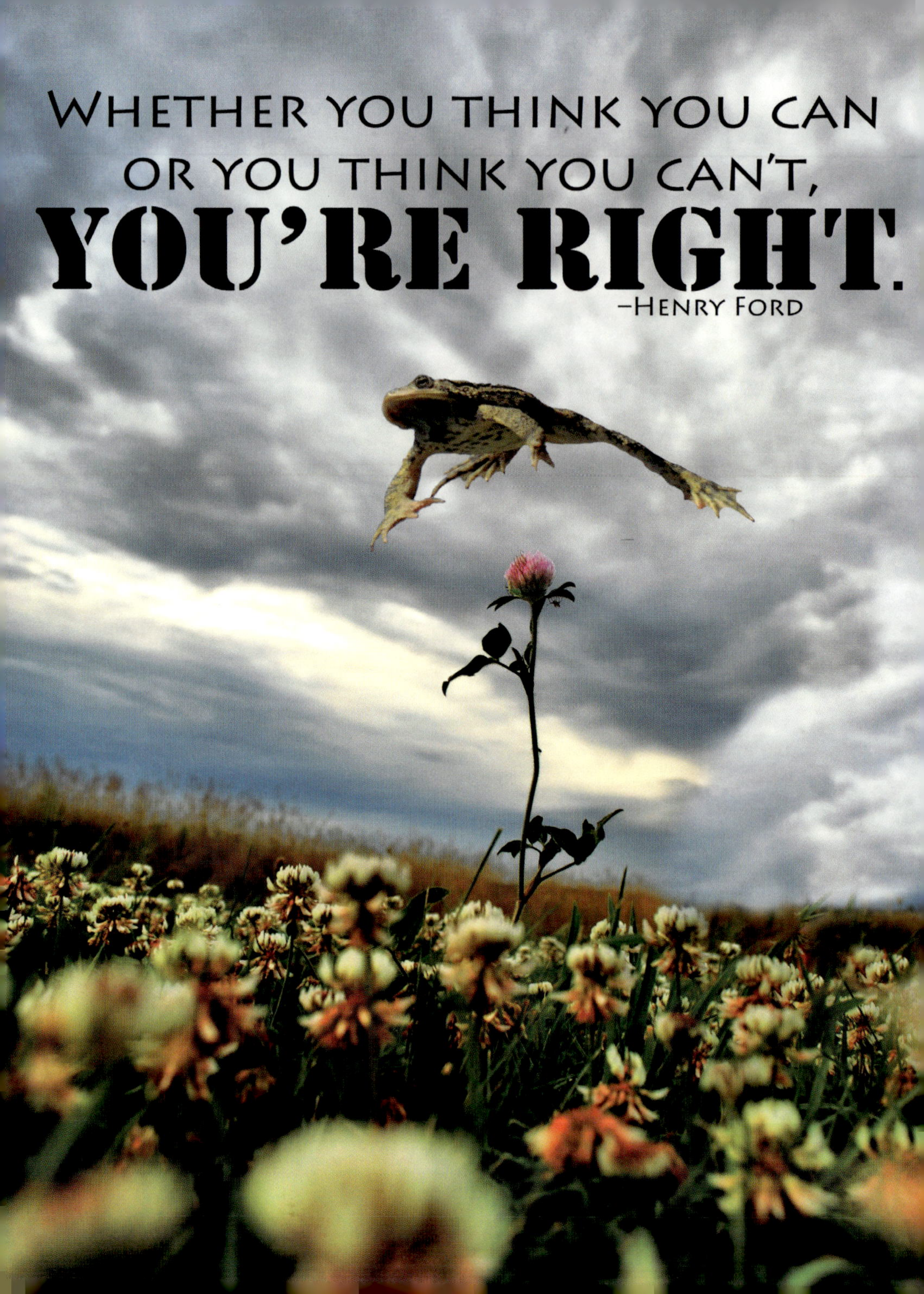

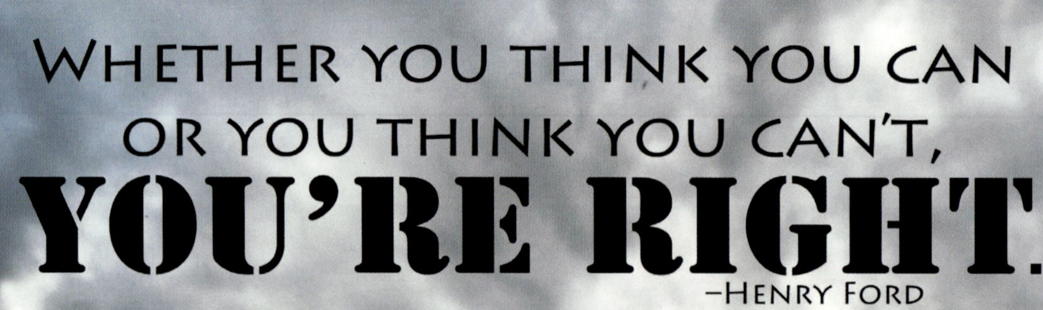
WHETHER YOU THINK YOU CAN
OR YOU THINK YOU CAN'T,
YOU'RE RIGHT.
–HENRY FORD

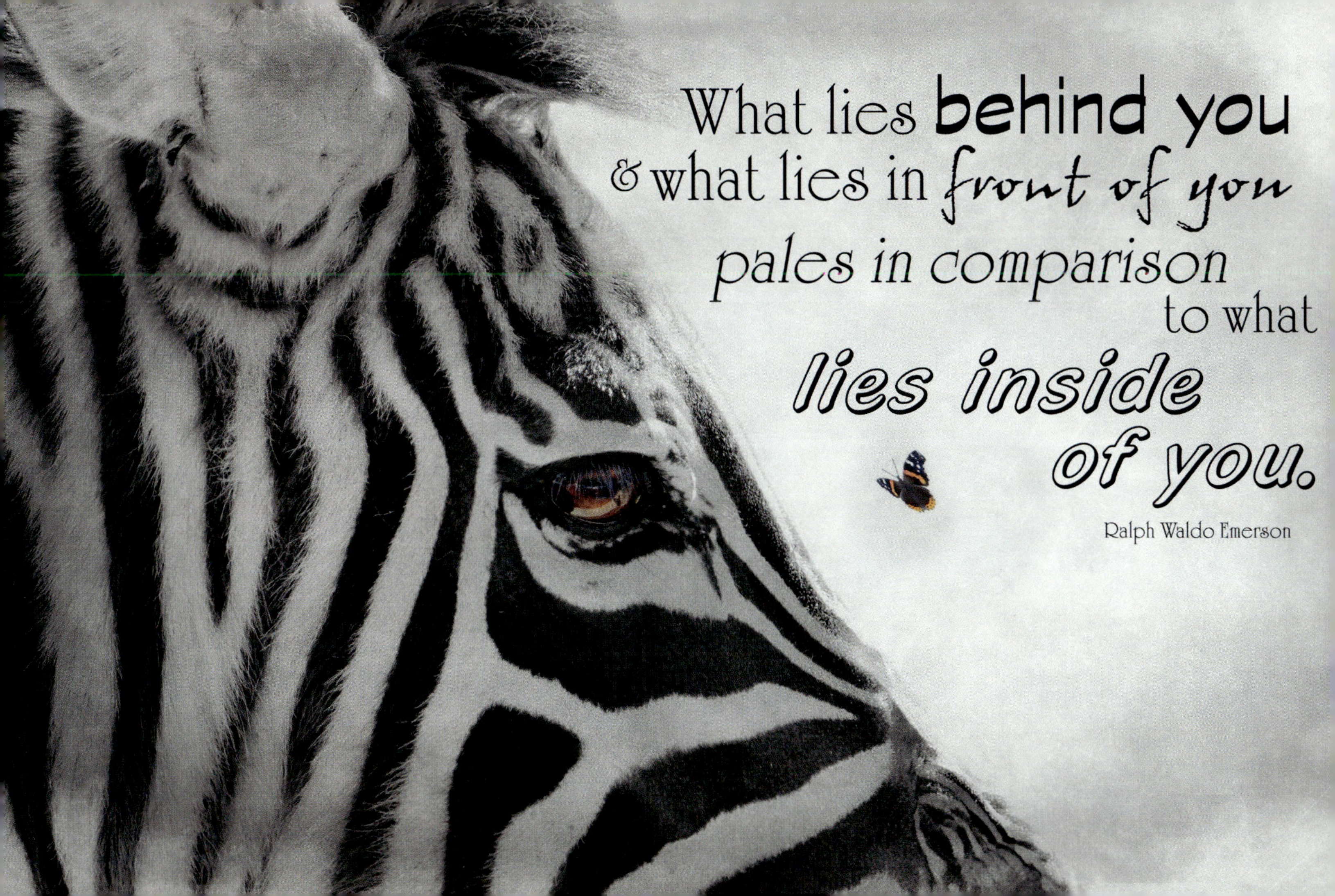
What lies behind you
& what lies in front of you
pales in comparison
to what
lies inside
of you.
Ralph Waldo Emerson

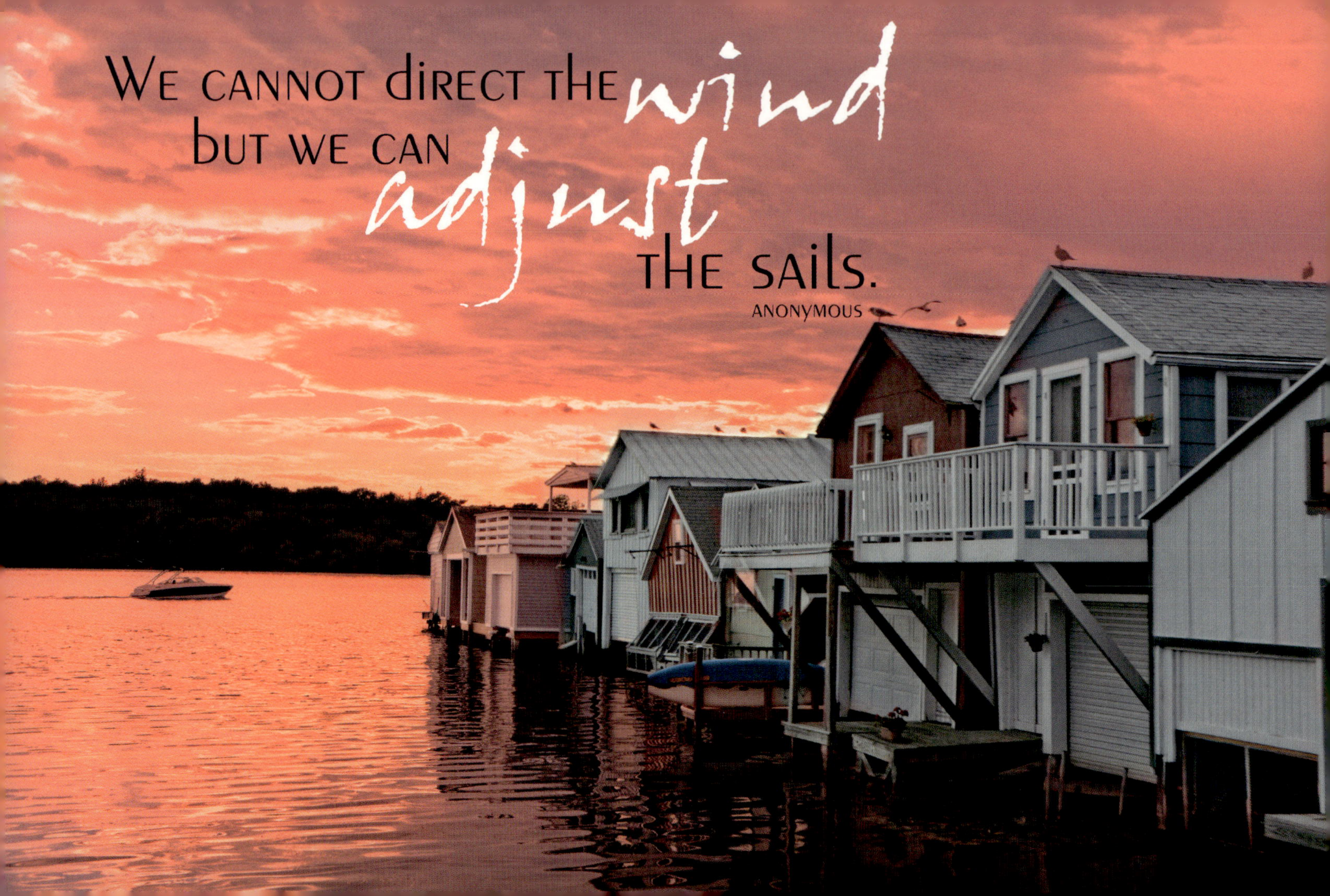

We cannot direct the wind
but we can adjust
the sails.
ANONYMOUS

Our greatest weakness
lies in giving up.
The most certain way to

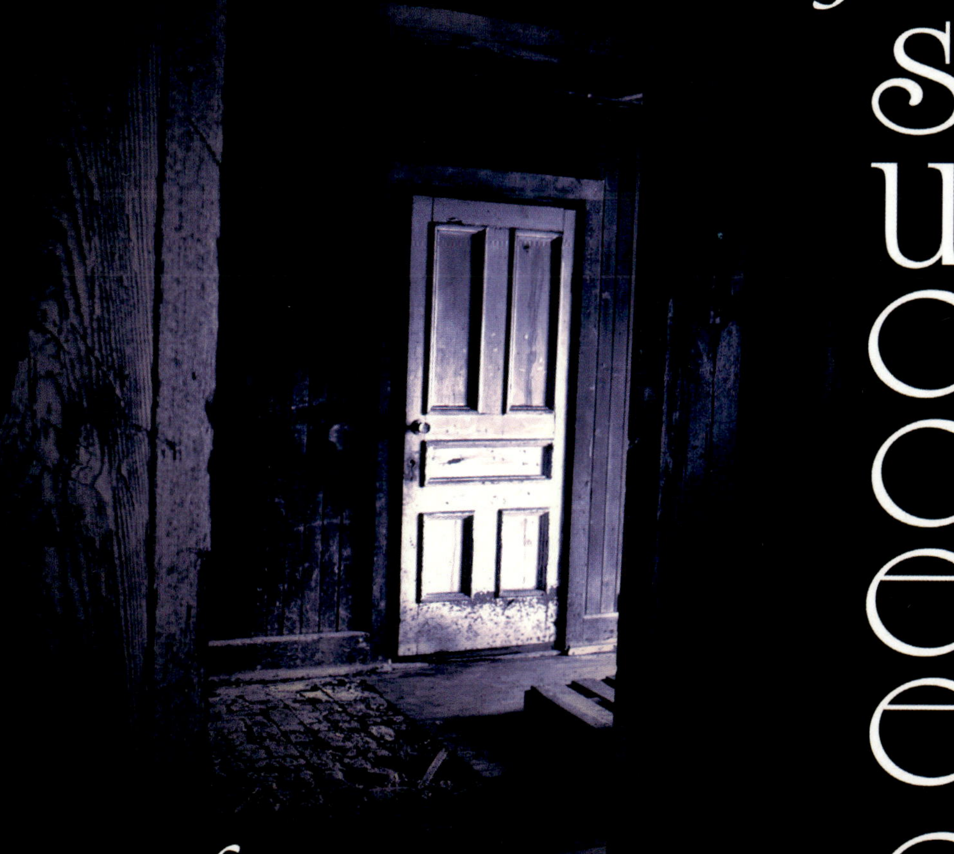

succeed
is always to try just
one
more
time.

Thomas A Edison

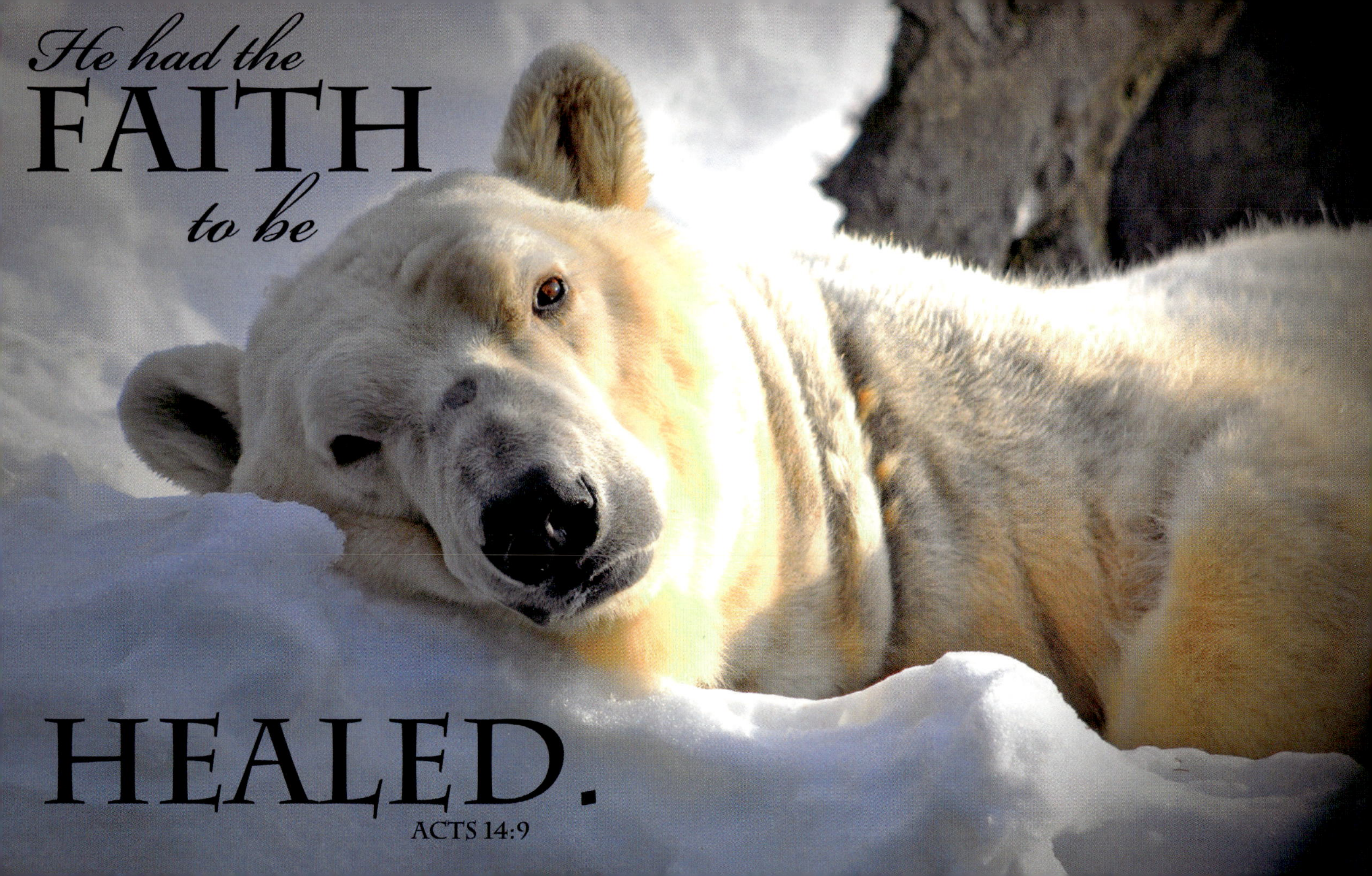
He had the
FAITH
to be
HEALED.
ACTS 14:9

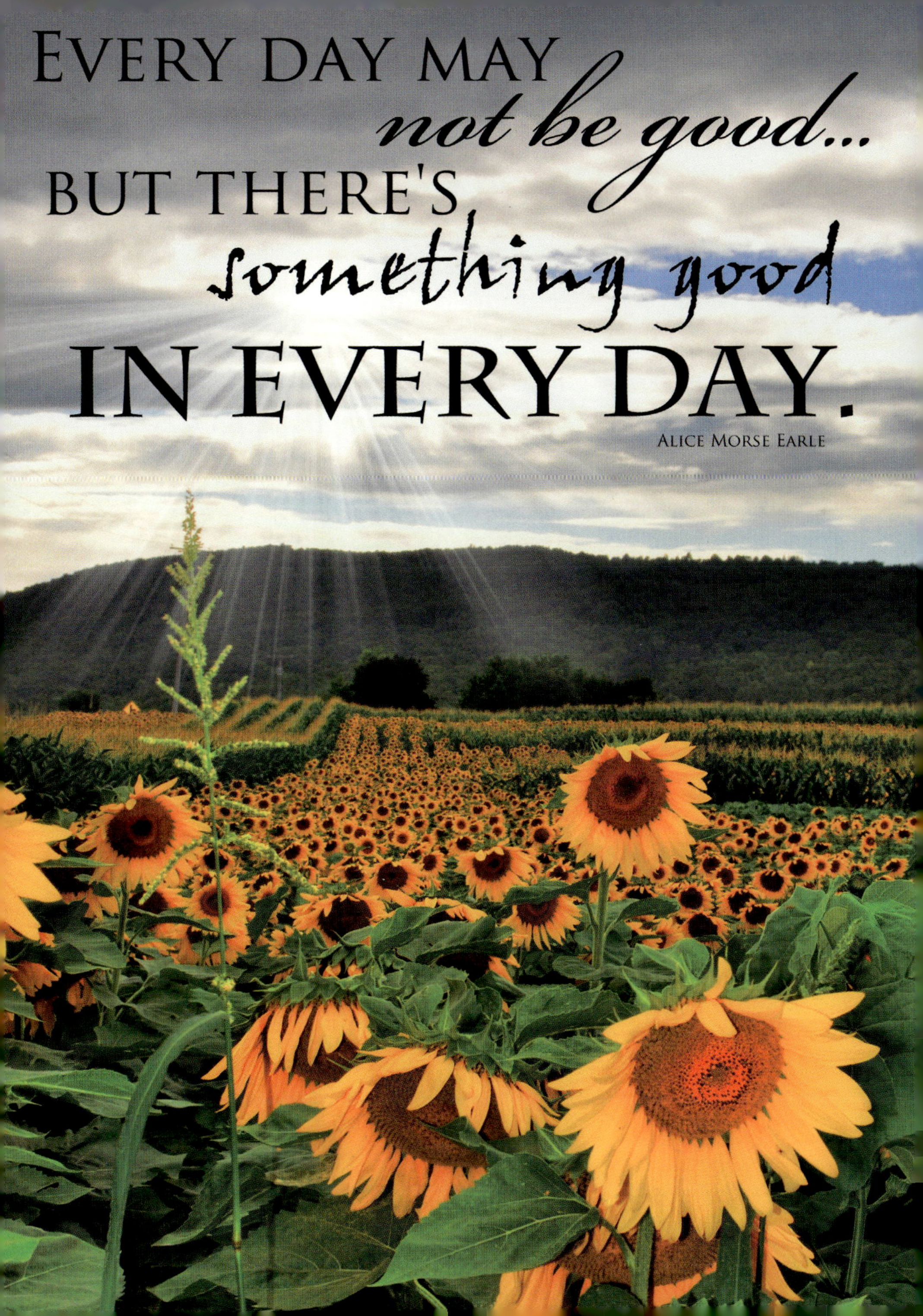

EVERY DAY MAY *not be good...*
BUT THERE'S *something good*
IN EVERY DAY.

ALICE MORSE EARLE

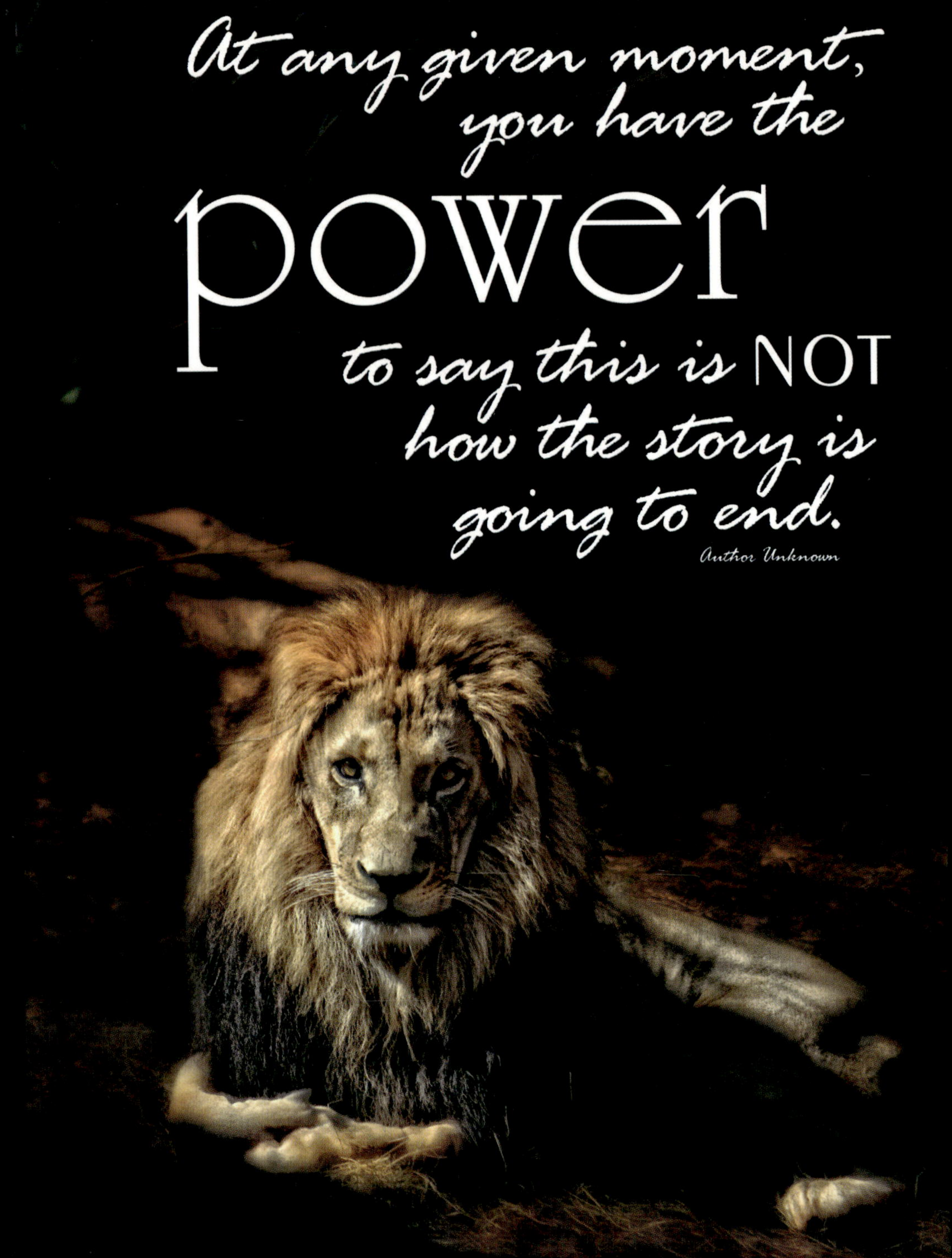
At any given moment,
you have the
power
to say this is NOT
how the story is
going to end.
Author Unknown

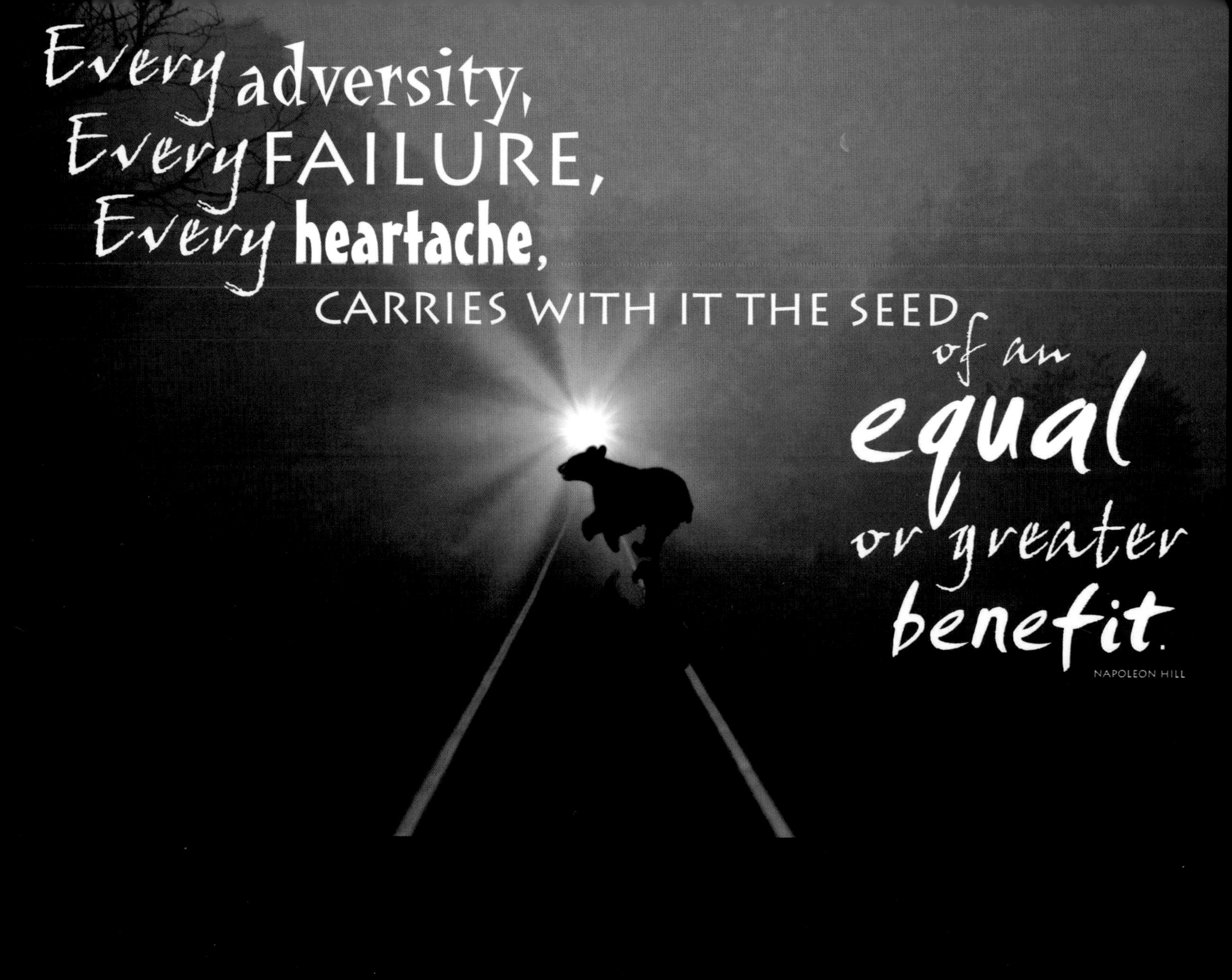

Every adversity,
Every FAILURE,
Every **heartache**,
CARRIES WITH IT THE SEED
of an
equal
or greater
benefit.

NAPOLEON HILL

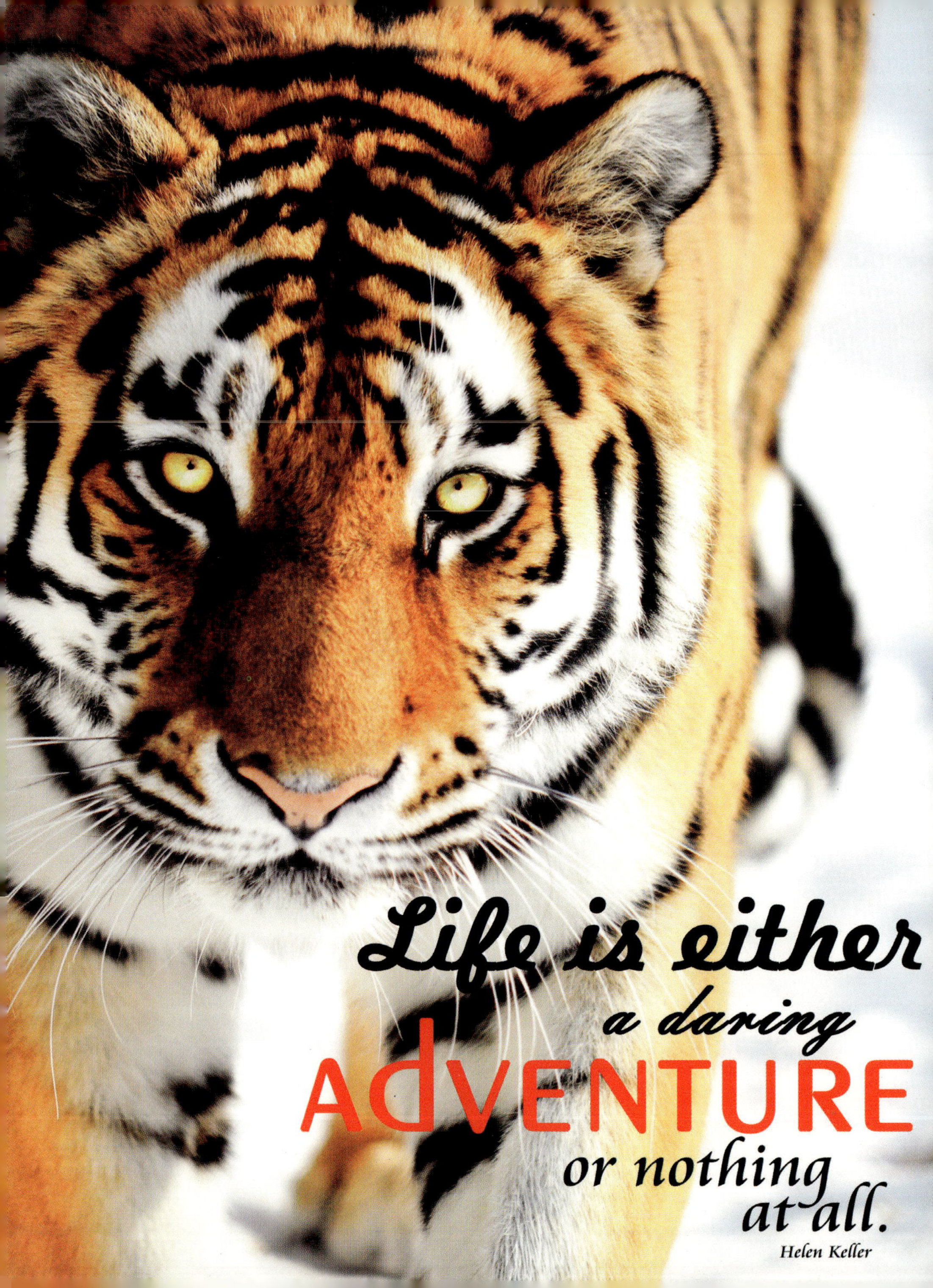
Life is either
a daring
ADVENTURE
or nothing
at all.
Helen Keller

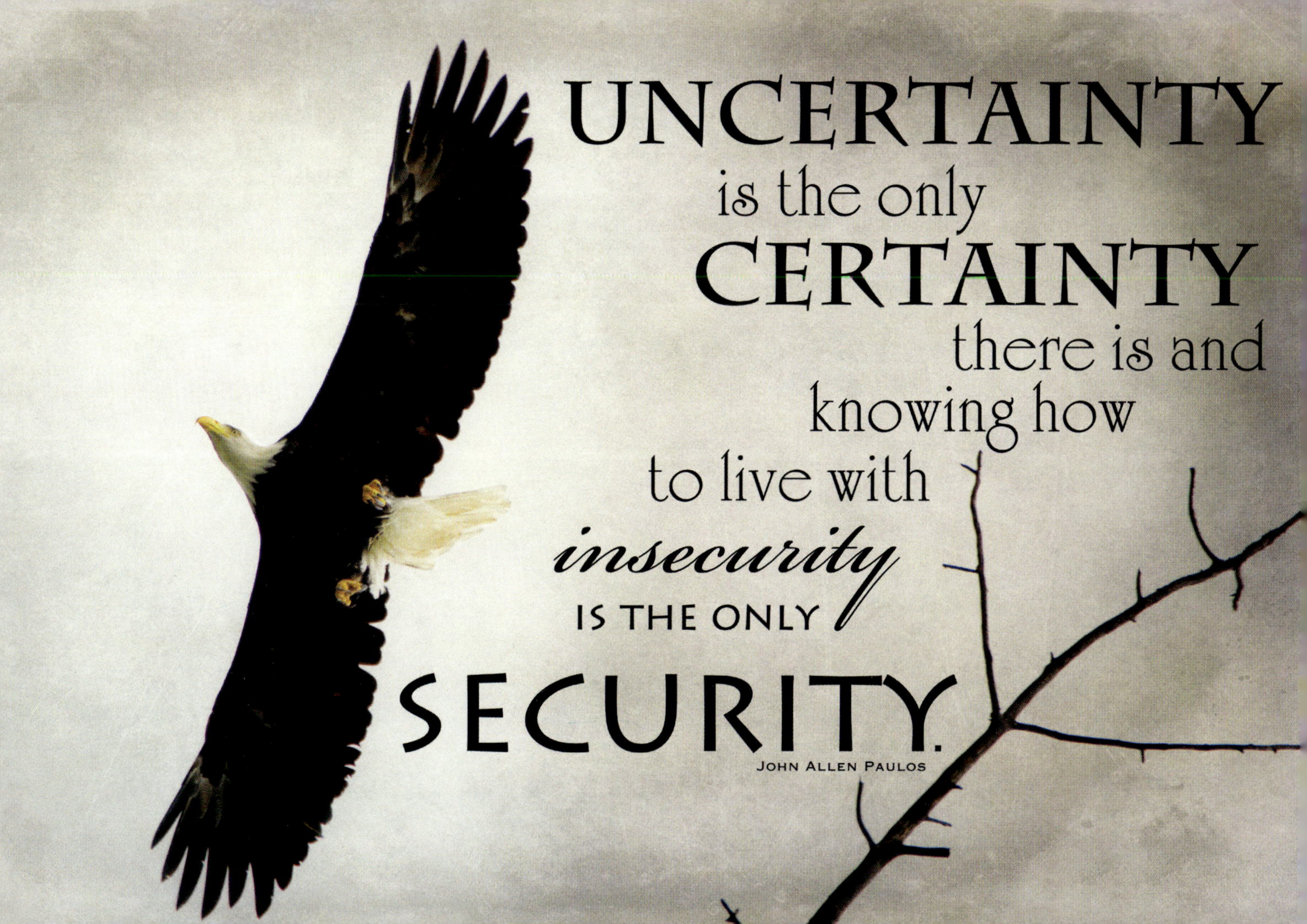
UNCERTAINTY
is the only
CERTAINTY
there is and
knowing how
to live with
insecurity
IS THE ONLY
SECURITY.
JOHN ALLEN PAULOS

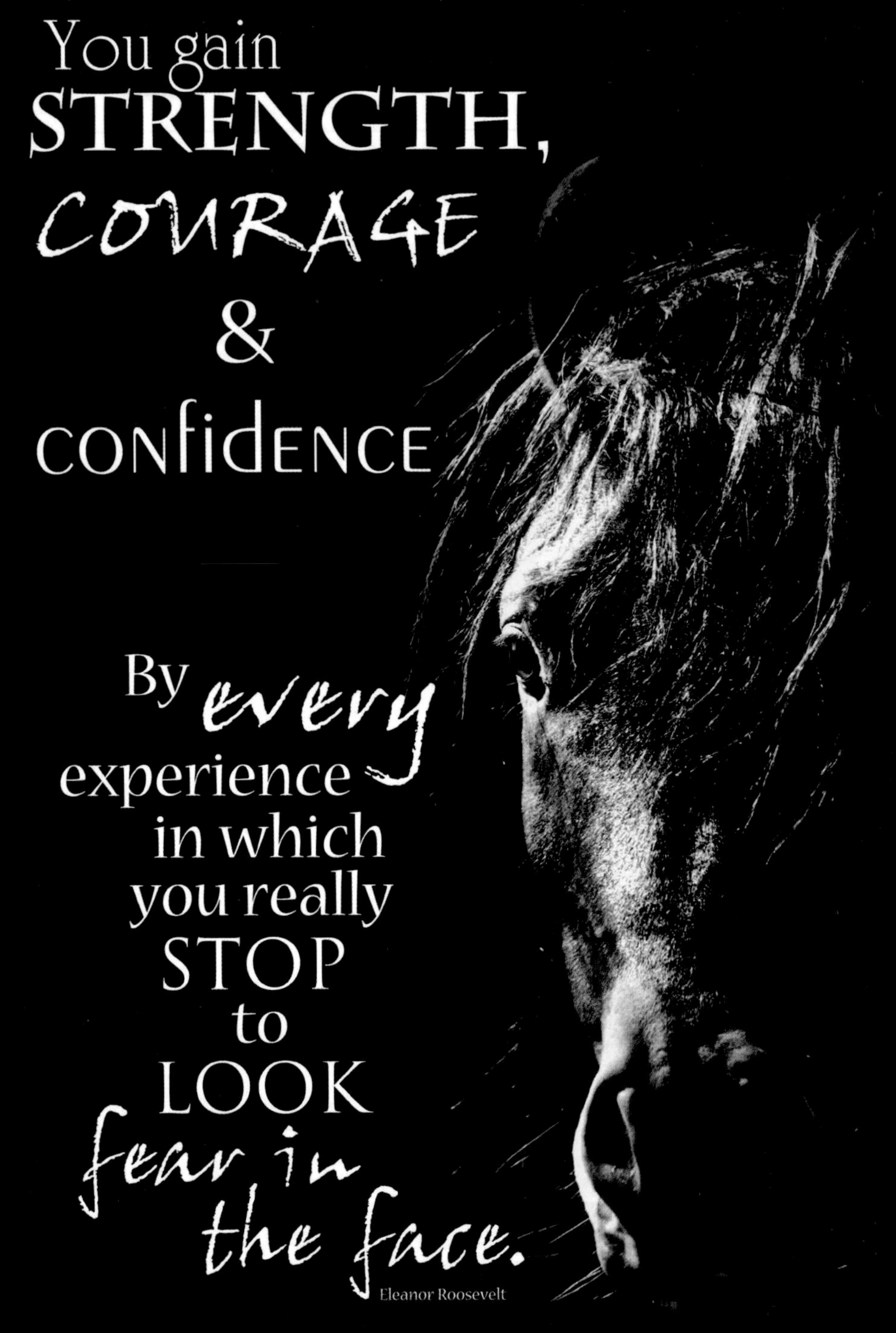
You gain
STRENGTH,
COURAGE
&
confidence
By every
experience
in which
you really
STOP
to
LOOK
fear in
the face.
Eleanor Roosevelt

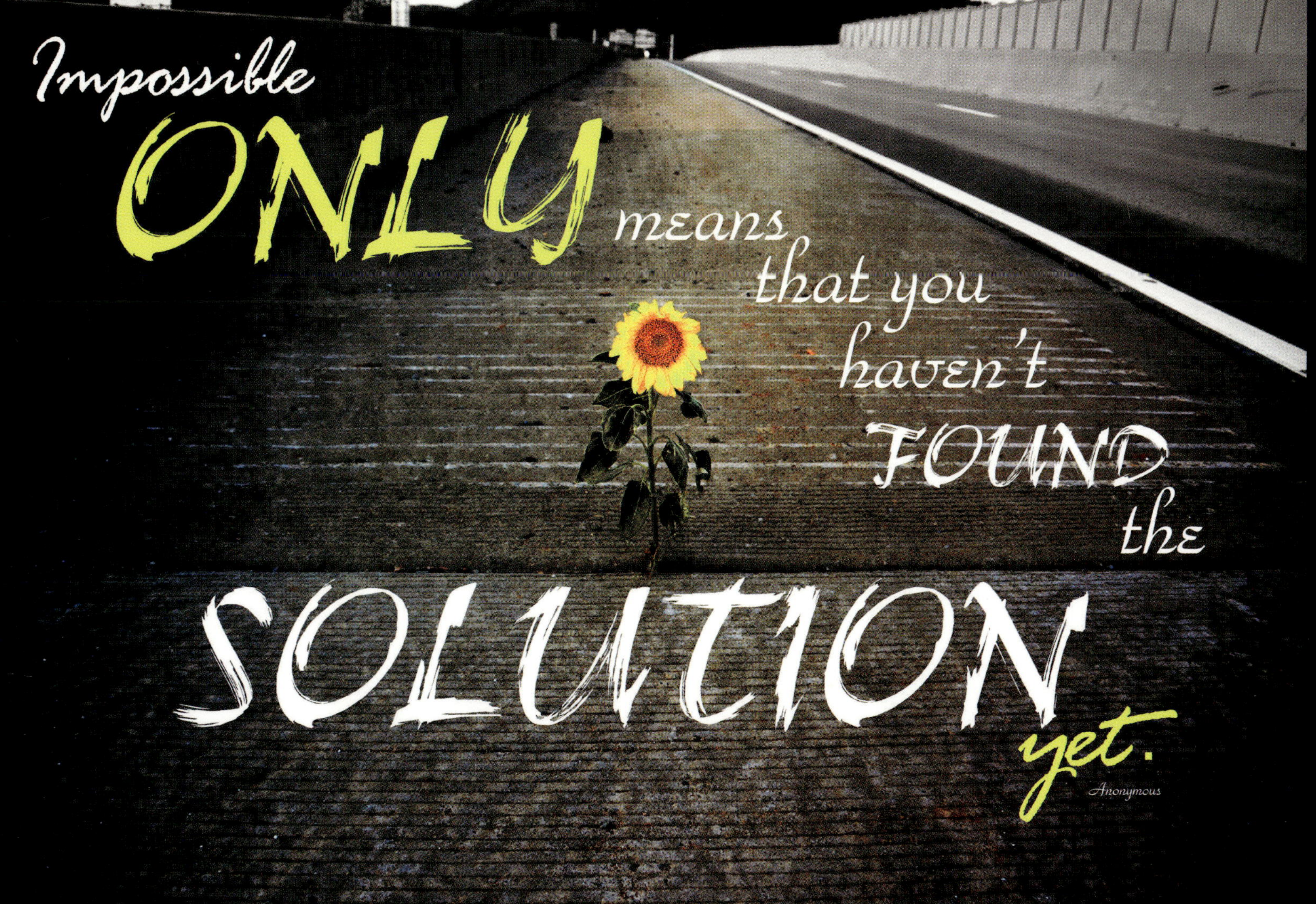
Impossible
ONLY means
that you
haven't
FOUND
the
SOLUTION
yet.
Anonymous

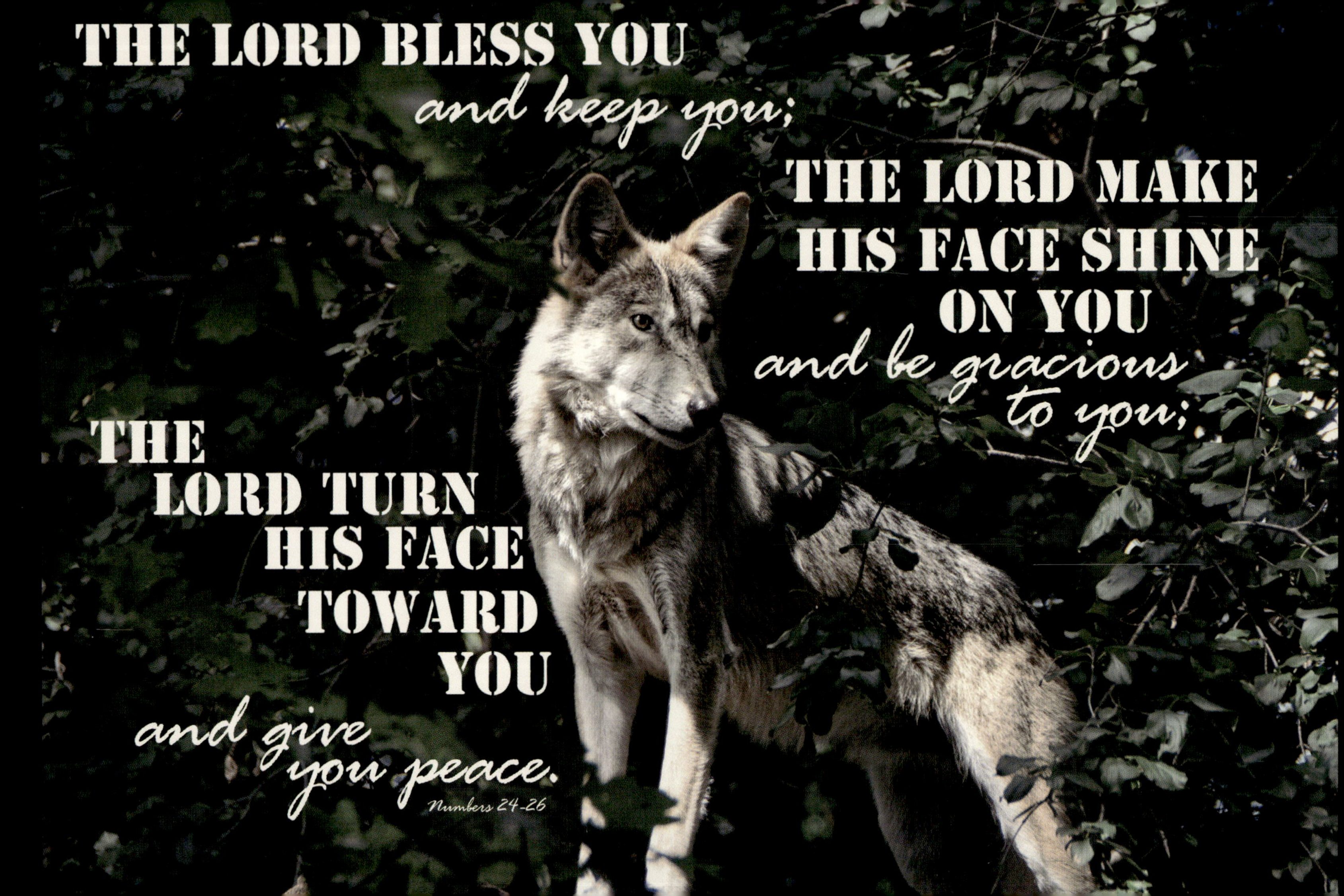
THE LORD BLESS YOU
and keep you;
THE LORD MAKE
HIS FACE SHINE
ON YOU
and be gracious
to you;
THE
LORD TURN
HIS FACE
TOWARD
YOU
and give
you peace.
Numbers 24-26

DO NOT GO
WHERE THE PATH
MAY LEAD,
*go instead where there
is no path and*
LEAVE A
TRAIL.

RALPH WALDO EMERSON

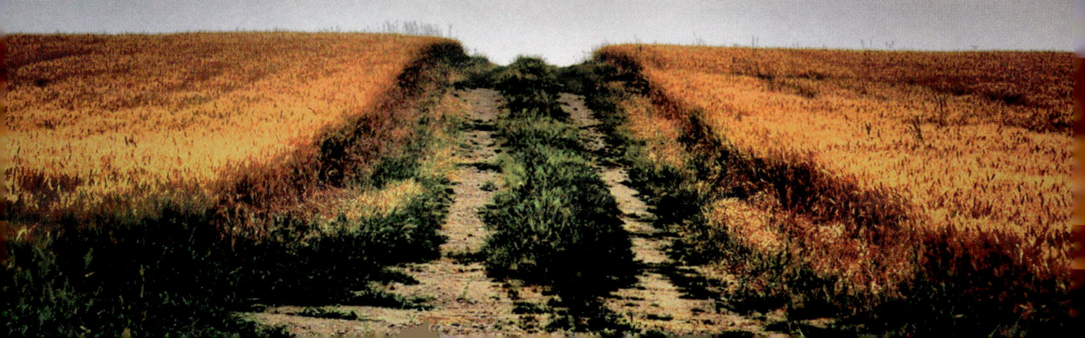

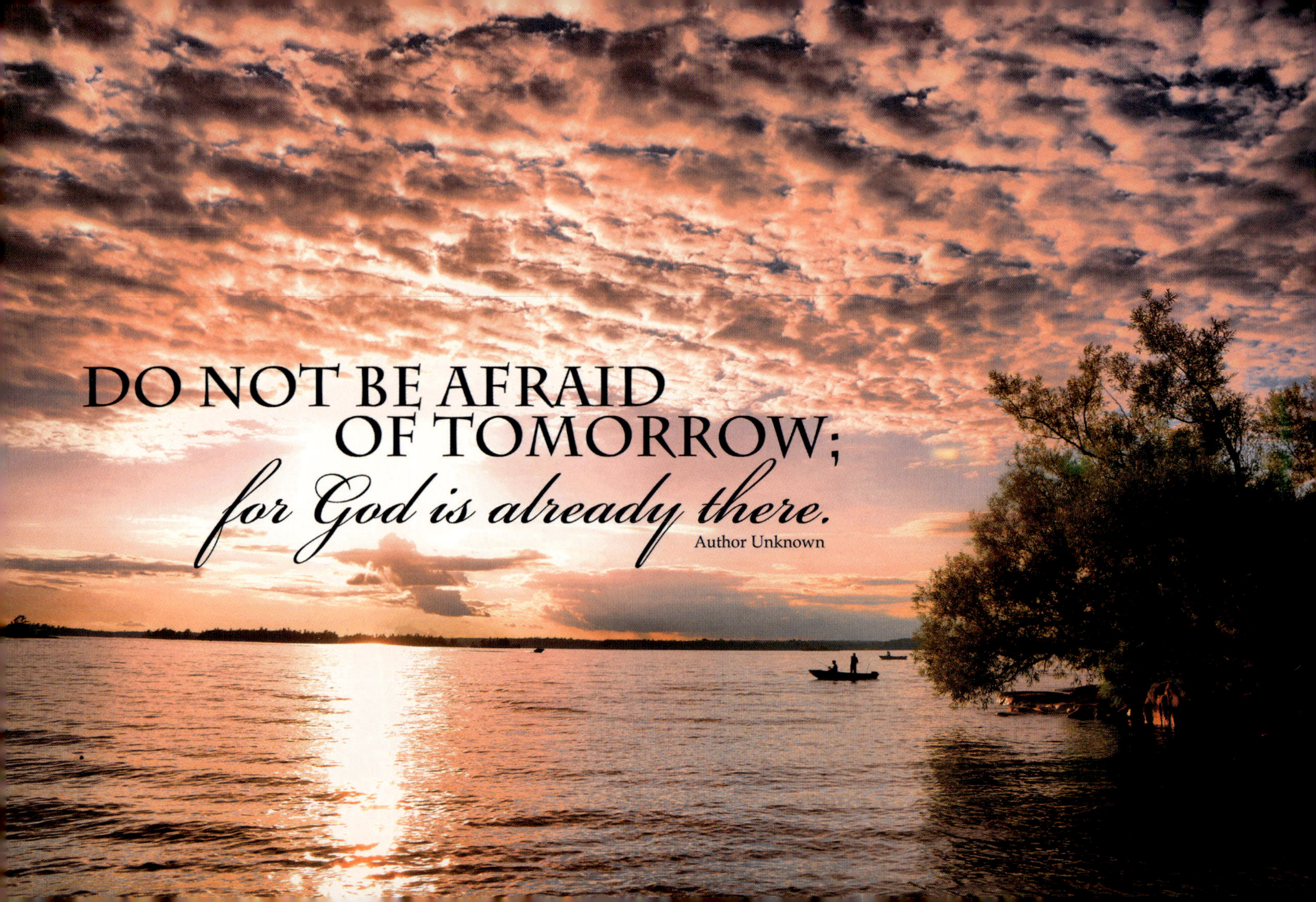
DO NOT BE AFRAID
OF TOMORROW;
for God is already there.
Author Unknown

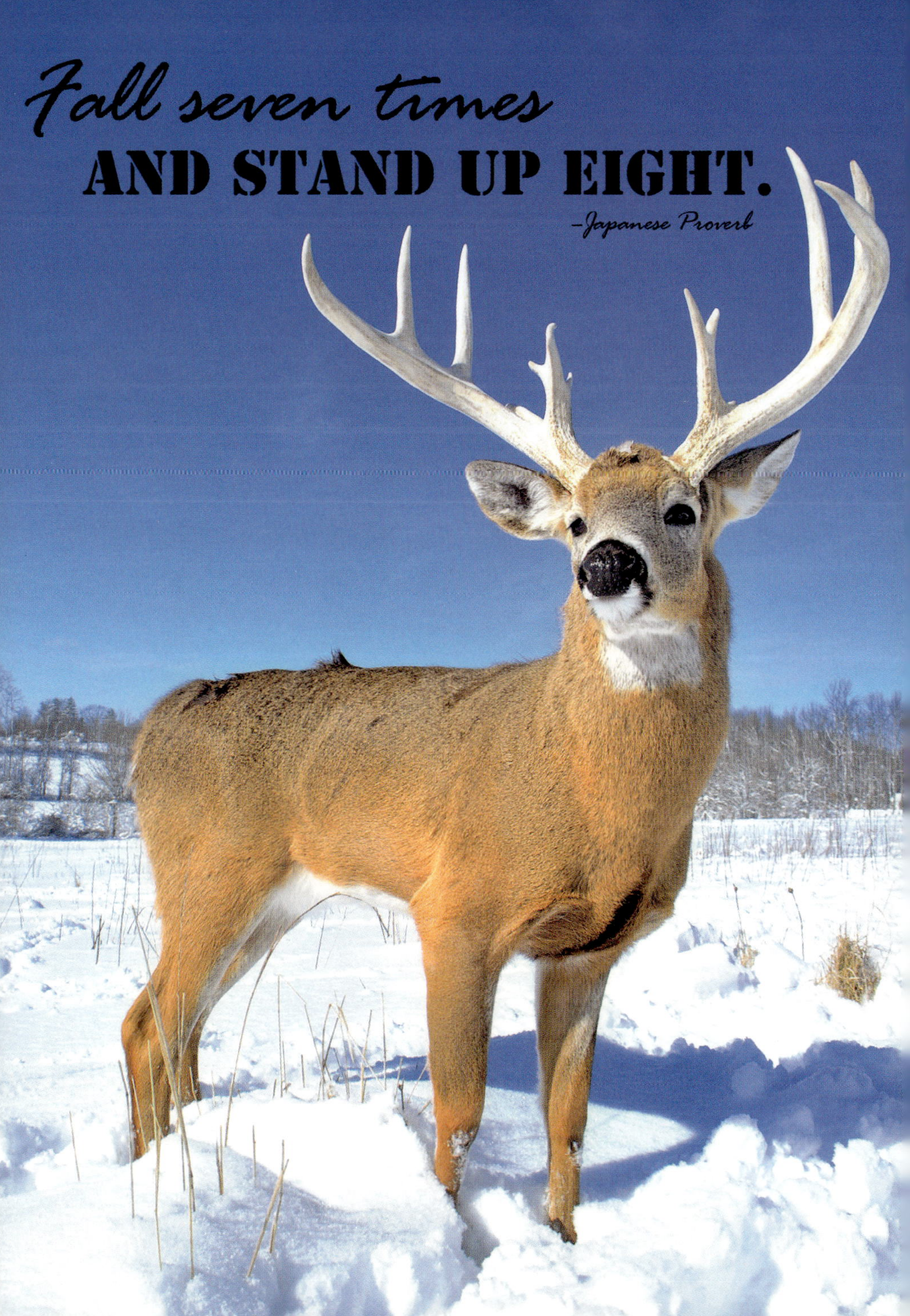
Fall seven times
AND STAND UP EIGHT.
–Japanese Proverb

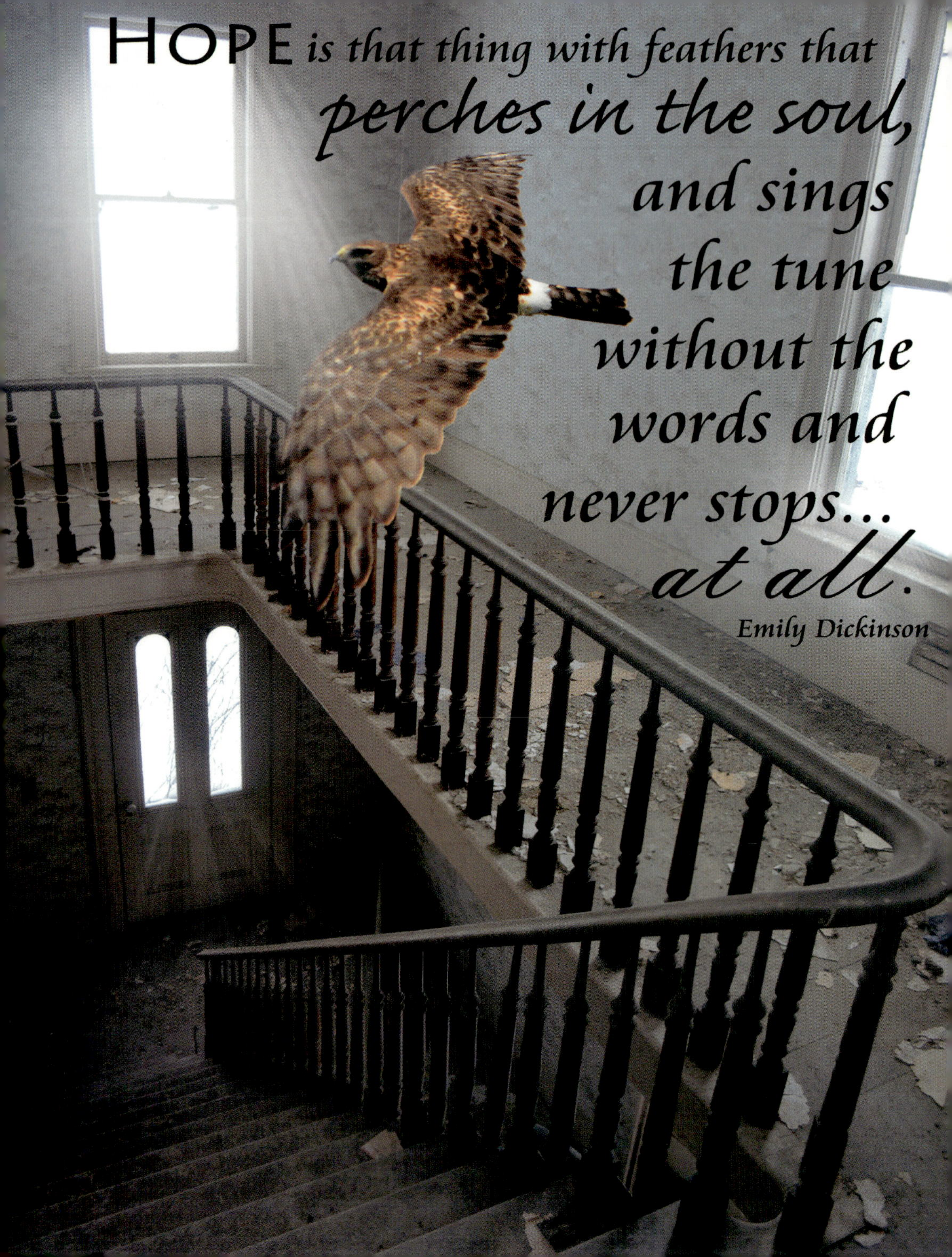
HOPE is that thing with feathers that
perches in the soul,
and sings
the tune
without the
words and
never stops...
at all.
Emily Dickinson

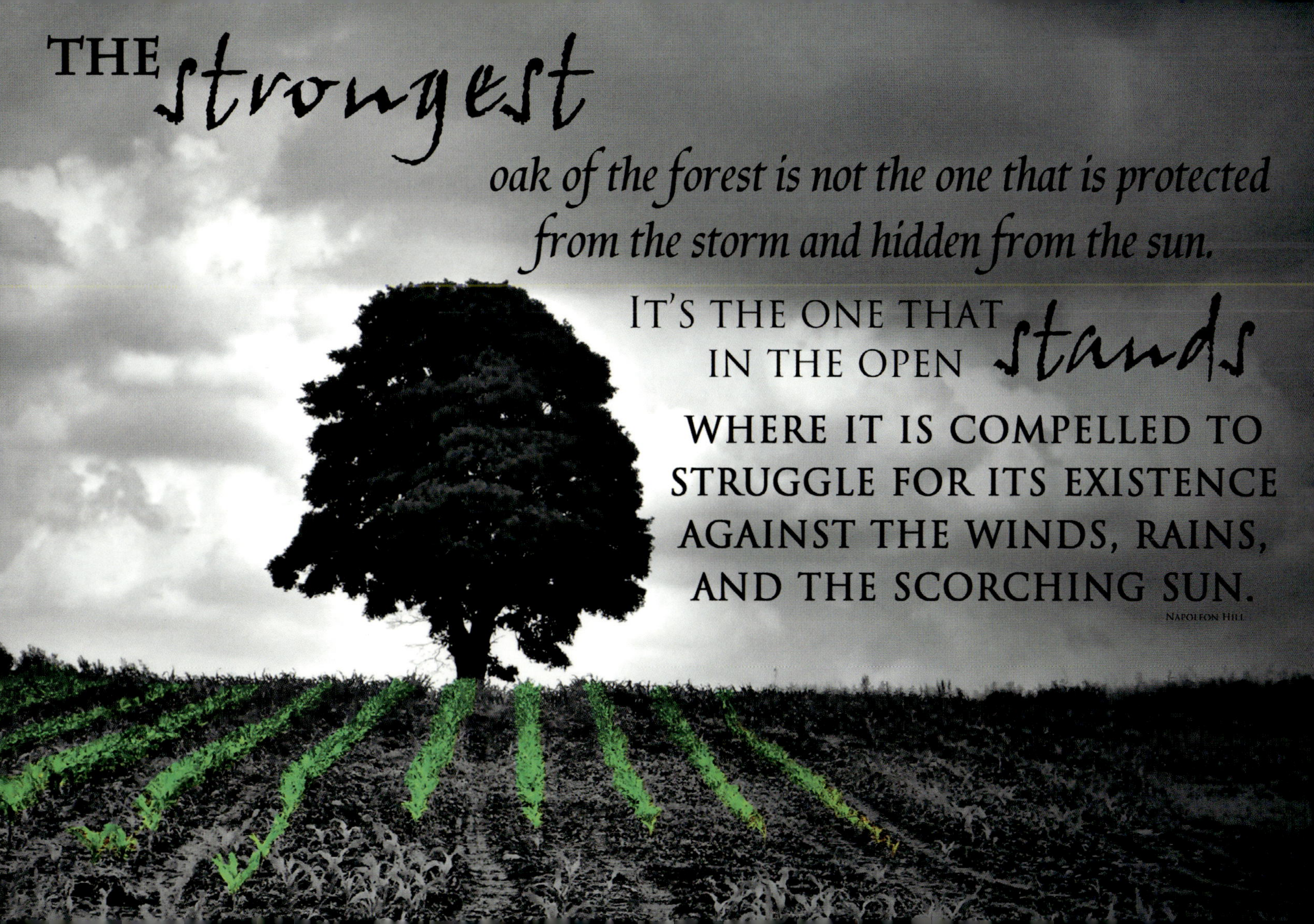
THE strongest
oak of the forest is not the one that is protected
from the storm and hidden from the sun.
IT'S THE ONE THAT
IN THE OPEN stands
WHERE IT IS COMPELLED TO
STRUGGLE FOR ITS EXISTENCE
AGAINST THE WINDS, RAINS,
AND THE SCORCHING SUN.
NAPOLEON HILL

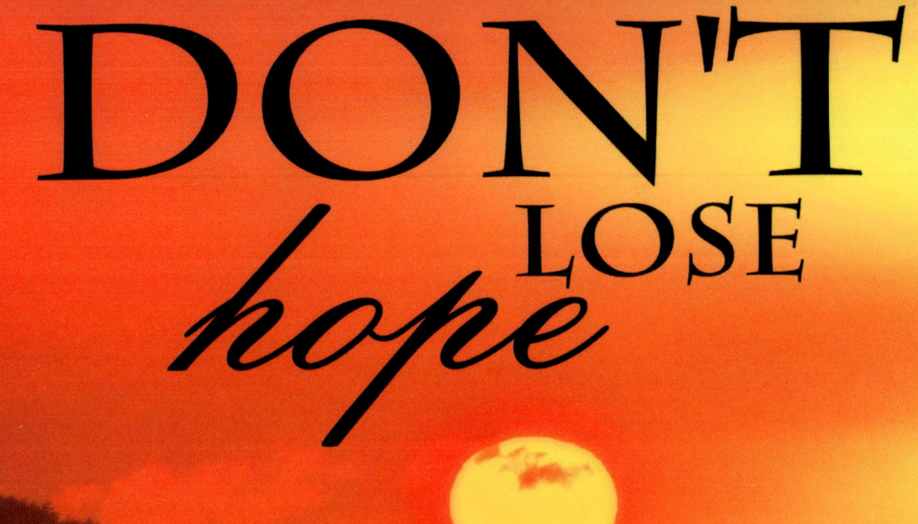
DON'T
LOSE
hope
WHEN THE SUN
GOES DOWN,
the STARS
come out.
UNKNOWN

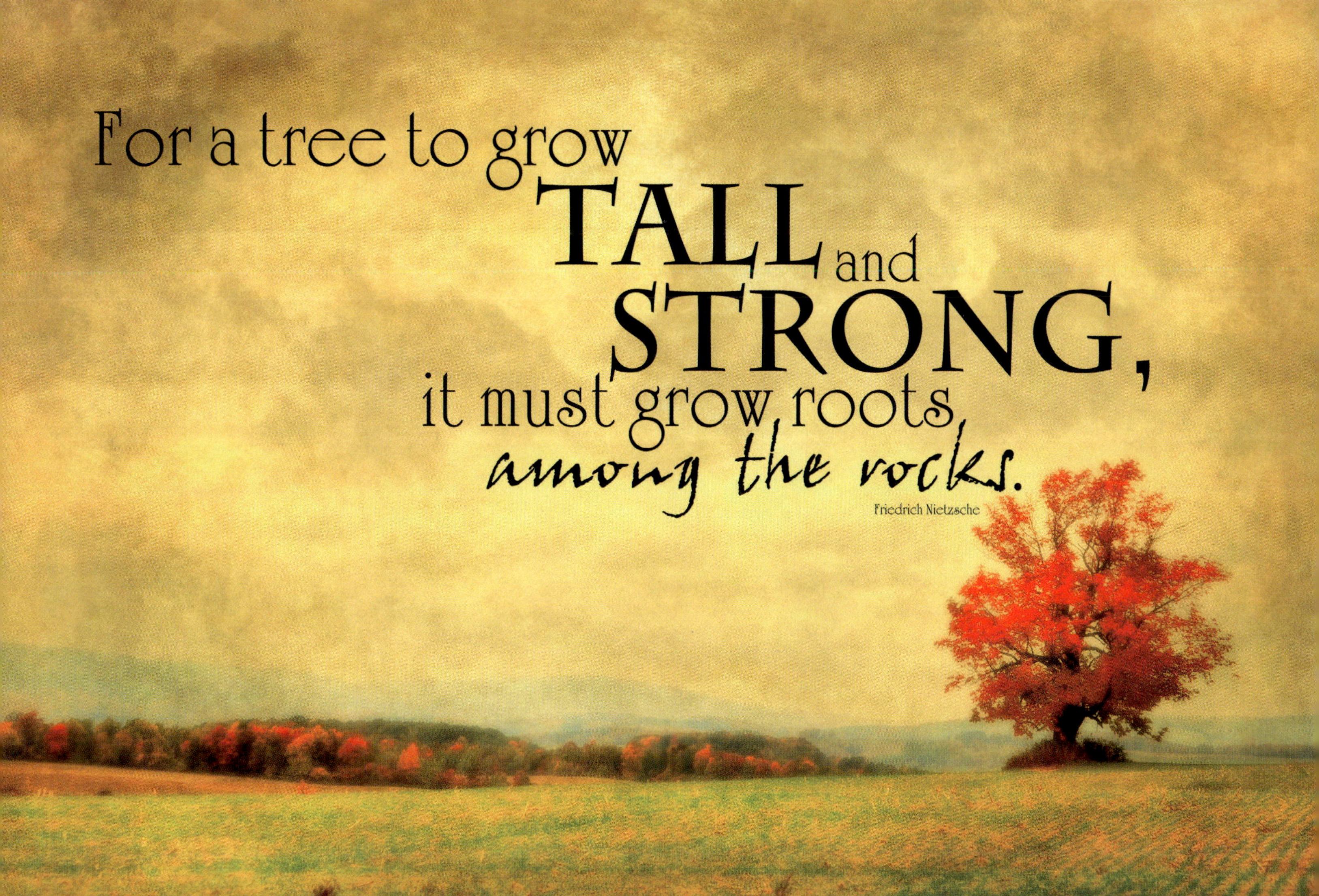
For a tree to grow
TALL and
STRONG,
it must grow roots
among the rocks.
Friedrich Nietzsche

EITHER YOU DECIDE TO STAY

in the shallow end of the pool

OR YOU GO OUT INTO THE

ocean.

CHRISTOPHER REEVE

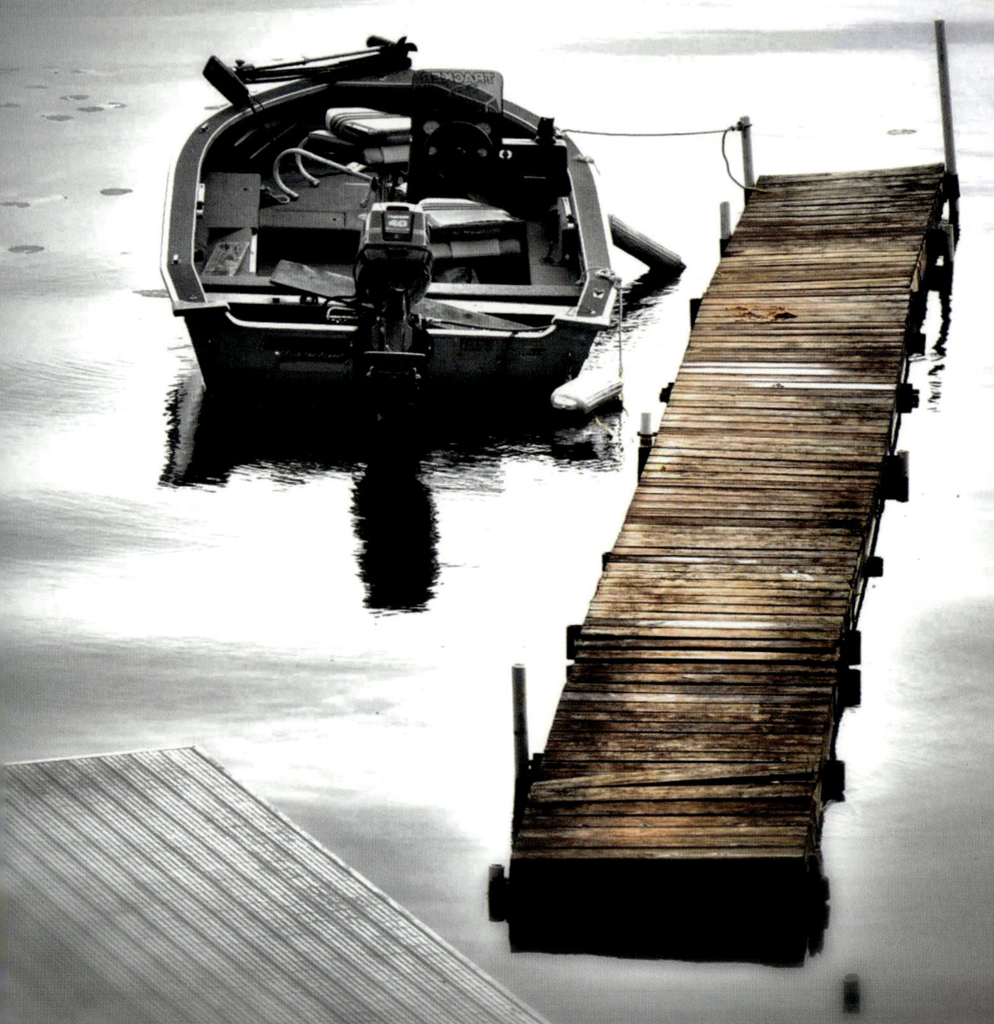

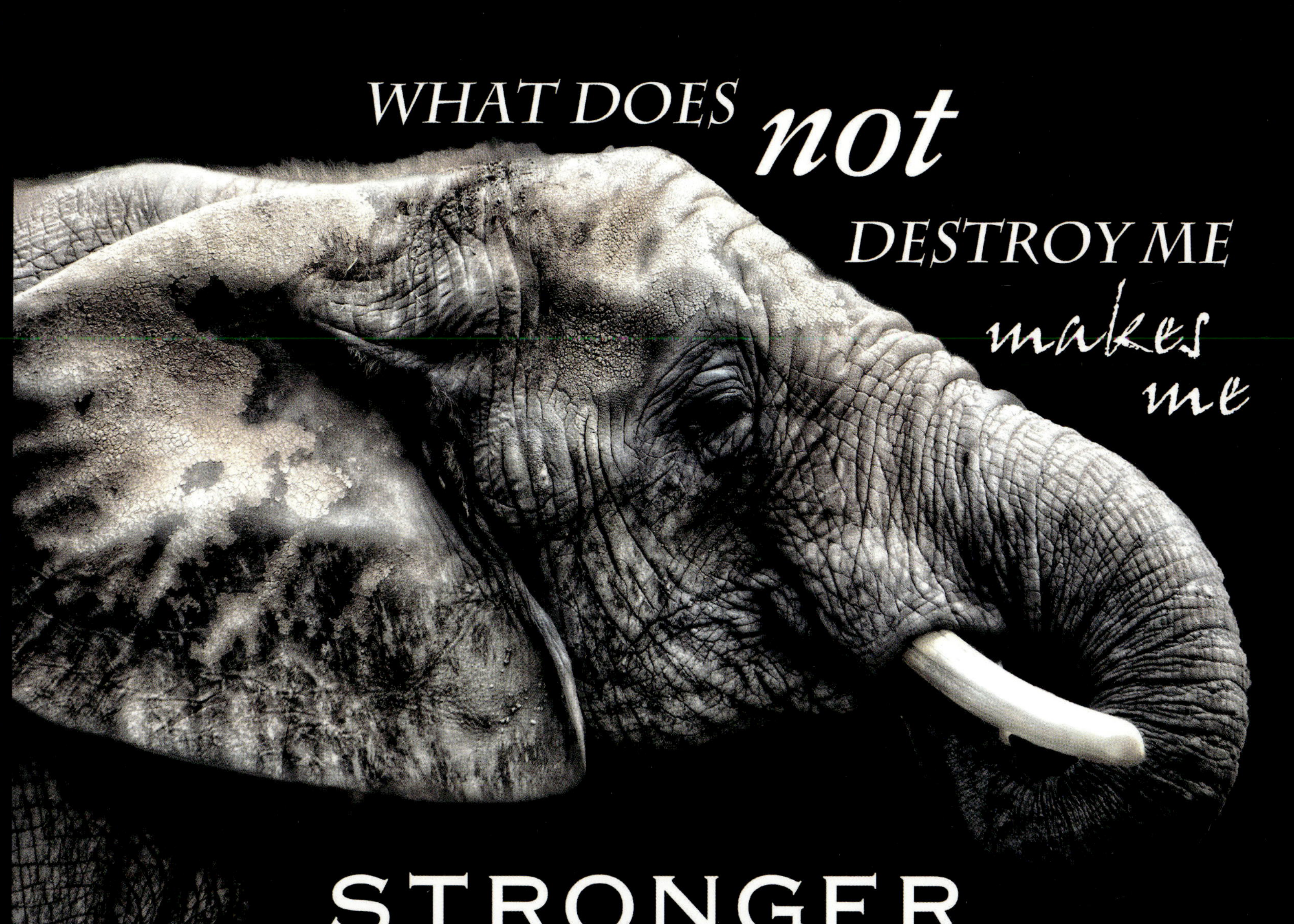
WHAT DOES not
DESTROY ME
makes
me
STRONGER.
FRIEDRICH NIETZSCHE

What Cancer Cannot Do –

Cancer is so *limited*...

It cannot cripple love,

It cannot shatter hope,

It cannot corrode faith,

It cannot destroy peace,

It cannot kill friendship,

It cannot suppress memories,

It cannot silence courage,

It cannot invade the soul,

It cannot steal eternal life,

It cannot conquer the spirit.

Author Unknown

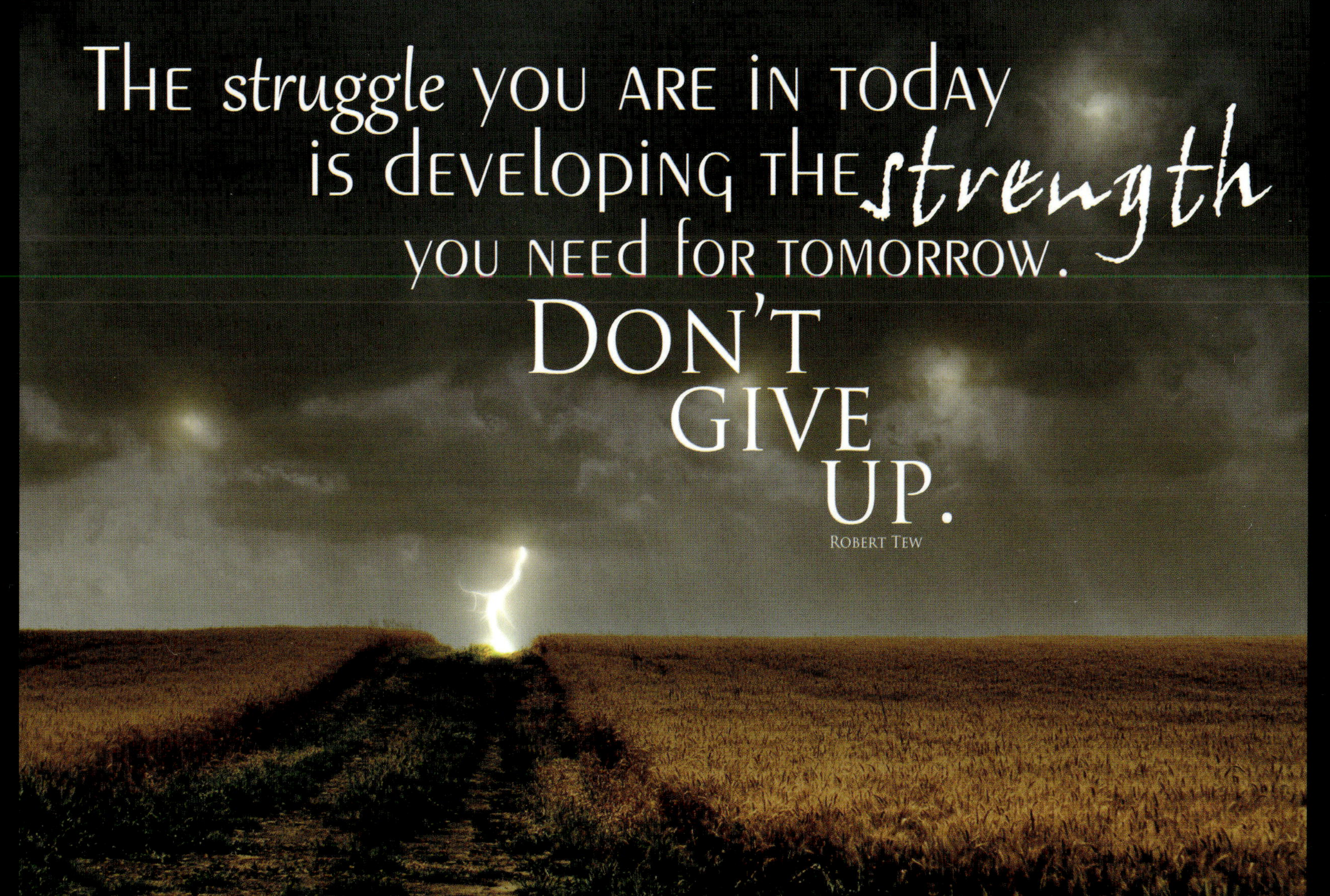
The struggle you are in today
is developing the strength
you need for tomorrow.
Don't
give
up.
Robert Tew

Acknowledgments:

Thanks to the following authors/foundations who gave me permission to utilize their quotes for this book. All other quotes used were found to be in public domain.
(Listed in order that quote appears)

Dr. Nido Qubein

Nido is an international speaker and accomplished author on sales, communication, and leadership. In 2005 he accepted presidency of High Point University which has an enrollment of more than 4,000 undergraduate and graduate students. Dr. Qubein serves on several national and local boards, and is the recipient of numerous awards. He is also chairman of Great Harvest Bread Company with 220 stores in 43 states. For more information visit: www.nidoqubein.com and www.hightpoint.edu.

Mary Anne Radmacher

Learn more about Mary Anne at maryanneradmacher.net

Lance Armstrong

www.livestrong.org

Napoleon Hill Foundation

www.naphill.org

John Allen Paulos

https://math.temple.edu/paulos~/

Christopher & Dana Reeve Foundation

http://www.christopherreeve.org/

Kiss it CANCER

For ordering information please visit:

WWW.KISSITCANCER.COM